BATTLE ZONE NORMANDY

ROAD TO
FALAISE

The 'Battle Zone Normandy' Series

Orne Bridgehead Lloyd Clark

Sword Beach Ken Ford

Juno Beach Ken Ford

Gold Beach Simon Trew

Omaha Beach Stephen Badsey & Tim Bean

Utah Beach Stephen Badsey

Villers-Bocage George Forty

Battle for Cherbourg R.P.W. Havers

Operation Epsom Lloyd Clark

Battle for St-Lô Nigel de Lee

Battle for Caen Simon Trew & Stephen Badsey

Operation Cobra Christopher Pugsley

Road to Falaise Stephen Hart

Falaise Pocket Paul Latawski

All of these titles can be ordered via the
Sutton Publishing website
www.suttonpublishing.co.uk

The 'Battle Zone Normandy'
Editorial and Design Team

Series Editor Simon Trew

Senior Commissioning Editor Jonathan Falconer

Assistant Editor Nick Reynolds

Cover and Page Design Martin Latham

Editing and Layout Donald Sommerville

Mapping Map Creation Ltd

Photograph Scanning and Mapping Bow Watkinson

Index Michael Forder

Battle Zone Normandy

ROAD TO FALAISE

STEPHEN HART

Series Editor: Simon Trew
Foreword: John English

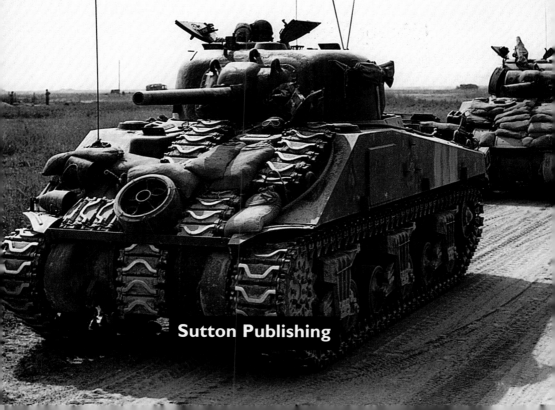

Sutton Publishing

First Published in 2004 by
Sutton Publishing Limited · Phoenix Mill
Thrupp · Stroud · Gloucestershire · GL5 2BU

Text Copyright © Stephen Hart 2004
Tour map overlays Copyright © Sutton
  Publishing
Tour base maps Copyright © Institut
  Géographique National, Paris
GSGS (1944) map overlays Copyright ©
  Sutton Publishing
GSGS (1944) base maps Copyright ©
  The British Library/Crown Copyright

British Library Cataloguing in Publication Data
A catalogue record for this book is available
from The British Library.

ISBN 0-7509-3016-0

While every effort has been made to ensure
that the information given in this book is
accurate, the publishers, the author and the
series editor do not accept responsibility for
any errors or omissions or for any changes in
the details given in this guide or for the
consequence of any reliance on the
information provided. The publishers would be
grateful if readers would advise them of any
inaccuracies they may encounter so these can
be considered for future editions of this book.
The inclusion of any place to stay, place to eat,
tourist attraction or other establishment in
this book does not imply an endorsement or
recommendation by the publisher, the series
editor or the author. Their details are included
for information only. Directions are for
guidance only and should be used in
conjunction with other sources of information.

Typeset in 10.5/14 pt Sabon

Printed and bound in England by
J.H. Haynes & Co. Ltd, Sparkford

Front cover: Canadian tanks advance across a dusty Normandy field during Operation 'Totalize'. *(National Archives of Canada [NAC] PA-128954)*

Page 1: The Polish Military Cemetery at Urville–Langannerie contains the graves of 587 soldiers killed during the liberation of Normandy. *(Author)*

Page 3: Canadian Shermans advance cautiously along a road near Cintheaux on the afternoon of 8 August 1944. *(NAC PA-114062)*

Page 7: During a lull in the battle, a Canadian NCO improvises a desk to write a letter home to his loved ones. *(NAC PA-191307)*

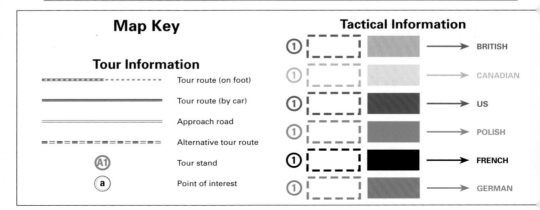

Map Key

Tour Information

.... Tour route (on foot)

———————— Tour route (by car)

———————— Approach road

=============== Alternative tour route

(A1) Tour stand

(a) Point of interest

Tactical Information

①   ⟶ BRITISH

①   ⟶ CANADIAN

①   ⟶ US

①   ⟶ POLISH

①   ⟶ FRENCH

①   ⟶ GERMAN

CONTENTS

THE NORMANDY BATTLEFIELD

Legend:
- ● Town
- Railway
- Road
- Caen Canal
- Département boundary
- Contour 100 metres
- Contour 200 metres
- Contour 300 metres

0   25   50
Kilometres

Bay of the Seine

Cherbourg

Valognes   ● Quineville
Montebourg
Ste. Mère Eglise   **UTAH**
Barneville

R. Douve

OMAHA   Port en Bessin   Arromanches   Courseulles   Le Havre

St. Laurent   **GOLD**   **JUNO**
Carentan   Isigny   *R. Aure*   **SWORD**
Bayeux   Ouistreham   Cabourg   Houlgate

Lessay   *R. Taute*
Périers   *R. Drôme*   *R. Seulles*   *R. Odon*   Caen   Argences   Lisie

MANCHE   St. Lô   Caumont   Mézidon

Coutances   *R. Vire*   Villers-Bocage   **CALVADOS**   *R. Dives*

Condé   Falaise

Granville   Vire   *R. Orne*   Argentan

Flers

Avranches   **ORNE**

Mortain   Domfront

R. Sélune

R. Mayenne

Fougères   Alenç

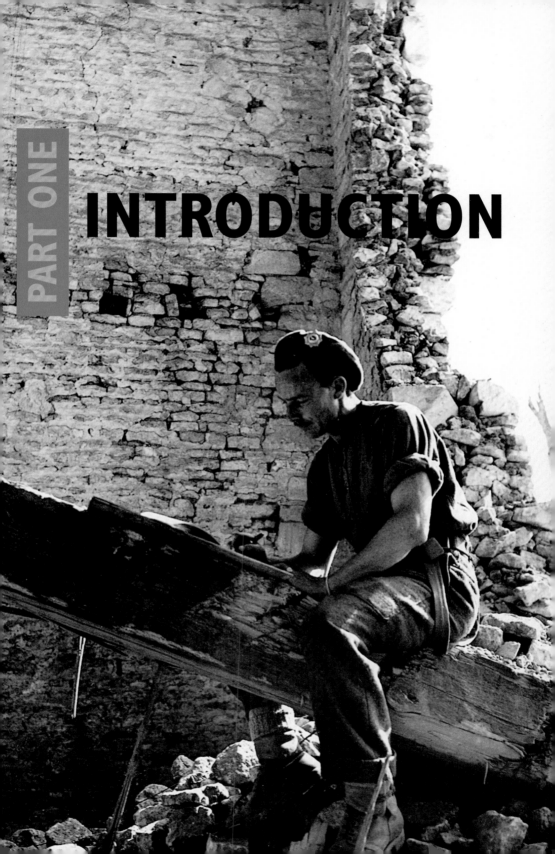

PART ONE

INTRODUCTION

BATTLE ZONE NORMANDY

The Battle of Normandy was one of the greatest military clashes of all time. From late 1943, when the Allies appointed their senior commanders and began the air operations that were such a vital preliminary to the invasion, until the end of August 1944, it pitted against one another several of the most powerful nations on earth, as well as some of their most brilliant minds. When it was won, it changed the world forever. The price was high, but for anybody who values the principles of freedom and democracy, it is difficult to conclude that it was one not worth paying.

I first visited Lower Normandy in 1994, a year after I joined the War Studies Department at the Royal Military Academy Sandhurst (RMAS). With the 50th anniversary of D-Day looming, it was decided that the British Army would be represented at several major ceremonies by one of the RMAS's officer cadet companies. It was also suggested that the cadets should visit some of the battlefields, not least to bring home to them the significance of why they were there. Thus, at the start of June 1994, I found myself as one of a small team of military and civilian directing staff flying with the cadets in a draughty and noisy Hercules transport to visit the beaches and fields of Calvados, in my case for the first time.

I was hooked. Having met some of the veterans and seen the ground over which they fought – and where many of their friends died – I was determined to go back. Fortunately, the Army encourages battlefield touring as part of its soldiers' education, and on numerous occasions since 1994 I have been privileged to return to Normandy, often to visit new sites. In the process I have learned a vast amount, both from my colleagues (several of whom are contributors to this series) and from my enthusiastic and sometimes tri-service audiences, whose professional insights and penetrating questions have frequently made me re-examine my own assumptions and prejudices. Perhaps inevitably, especially when standing in one of Normandy's beautifully-maintained Commonwealth War Graves Commission cemeteries, I have also found myself deeply moved by the critical events that took place there in the summer of 1944.

'Battle Zone Normandy' was conceived by Jonathan Falconer, Commissioning Editor at Sutton Publishing, in 2001. Why not, he suggested, bring together recent academic research – some of which challenges the general perception of what happened on and after 6 June 1944 – with a perspective based on familiarity with the ground itself? We agreed that the opportunity existed for a series that would set out to combine detailed and accurate narratives, based mostly on primary sources, with illustrated guides to the ground itself, which could be used either in the field (sometimes quite literally), or by the armchair explorer. The book in your hands is the product of that agreement.

The 'Battle Zone Normandy' series consists of 14 volumes, covering most of the major and many of the minor engagements that went together to create the Battle of Normandy. The first six books deal with the airborne and amphibious landings on 6 June 1944, and with the struggle to create the firm lodgement that was the prerequisite for eventual Allied victory. Five further volumes cover some of the critical battles that followed, as the Allies' plans unravelled and they were forced to improvise a battle very different from that originally intended. Finally, the last three titles in the series examine the fruits of the bitter attritional struggle of June and July 1944, as the Allies irrupted through the German lines or drove them back in fierce fighting. The series ends, logically enough, with the devastation of the German armed forces in the 'Falaise Pocket' in late August.

Whether you use these books while visiting Normandy, or to experience the battlefields vicariously, we hope you will find them as interesting to read as we did to research and write. Far from the inevitable victory that is sometimes represented, D-Day and the ensuing battles were full of hazards and unpredictability. Contrary to the view often expressed, had the invasion failed, it is far from certain that a second attempt could have been mounted. Remember this, and the significance of the contents of this book, not least for your life today, will be the more obvious.

Dr Simon Trew
Royal Military Academy Sandhurst
December 2003

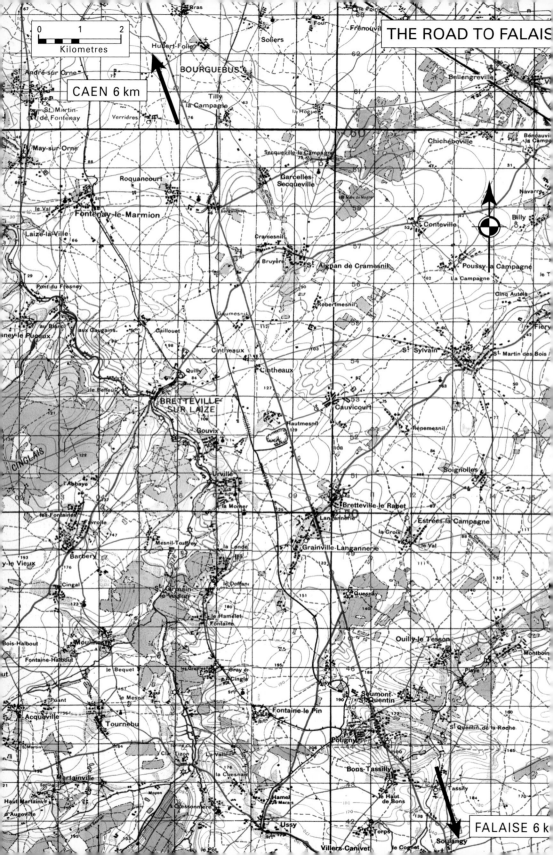

THE ROAD TO FALAIS

CAEN 6 km

FALAISE 6 k

FOREWORD

On 4 August 1944 General Montgomery directed the First Canadian Army to attack from the Caen sector in the direction of Falaise no later than 8 August. The object of this operation was to cut off the enemy forces facing Second British Army. The magnitude of the undertaking and the historic nature of the date were not lost upon the Canadians who clearly hoped to deliver an attack as decisive as that launched by the Canadian Corps at Amiens on 8 August 1918.

Operation 'Totalize' was essentially the brainchild of General Guy G. Simonds, the most battle-experienced commander in Canada's army. Arguably, Simonds remains second only to the Canadian Corps commander of the World War I, Sir Arthur Currie, in the pantheon of outstanding high-level officers produced by Canada. Like Currie, he was highly respected for his competence despite a hot temper and icy demeanour. Simonds never inspired troops, but by all accounts would have gotten on well with the likes of the operationally brilliant yet severe Field Marshal Erich von Manstein. As pointed out by Stephen Hart, Montgomery considered Simonds and Sir Brian Horrocks to be the two best corps commanders in 21st Army Group. Simonds was only 41 when he assumed command of II Canadian Corps in January 1944. In comparison, the youngest American corps commander was seven years older than Simonds, and of German corps commanders less than two per cent were under 45.

II Canadian Corps had already been blooded in Operation 'Atlantic', a flanking action in support of Operation 'Goodwood', the major attack executed by the British VIII Corps on 18 July 1944. Simonds' attempt to exploit the hard-won success of Atlantic foundered on poor tank–infantry cooperation and the arrival of German reserves, especially the 1st SS Panzer Division *Leibstandarte*. The subsequent attack on Verrières Ridge during Operation 'Spring' on 25 July, which resulted in the virtual annihilation of the Black Watch, also sullied Simonds' reputation. Yet both of these actions were mainly divisional as opposed to corps-executed operations. To a large extent, Simonds was let down by his divisional commanders. Maj-Gen Charles Foulkes of 2nd Division, for example, not only mixed up his manoeuvre brigades, when they should have fought together as they had trained, but never went forward to get a grip on the battle. On the other hand, while most actions foundered on the shoals of inadequate tank–infantry and artillery coordination, the striking success of the Royal Hamilton Light Infantry in ultimately taking and holding Verrières attested to what could have been done.

After two such bloody noses it is not surprising that Simonds chose to mount a major corps attack, if only to show his subordinates how to implement a proper fire plan. In Operation Totalize he cracked the German line wide open through the innovative use of armoured personnel carriers in a night operation. Failure to realize that the *Leibstandarte* had slipped away to participate in the German counter-attack at Mortain, regrettably caused Simonds to wait for a bomber strike on locations he incorrectly believed were German in-depth positions. To make matters worse, the 1st Polish and 4th Canadian Armoured Divisions, slated to exploit success, failed to make significant headway. The 4th Armoured, in particular, did not make sufficient use of its allotted artillery to blast its way forward. The commander of the spearhead 4th Armoured Brigade, who possessed adequate means to coordinate artillery fire for units, also abrogated responsibility to his tank-infantry battle groups. Both he and his divisional commander could have done much more to 'stage manage' the operation. In one of the few *Hitlerjugend* actions in Normandy where tanks played a greater role than anti-tank guns, Totalize was halted. A break-through had been accomplished, but not a breakout, though Totalize more than any other factor may have accelerated the German withdrawal from Mortain.

We are nonetheless thus left to ponder that, had the II Canadian Corps in the early morning of 8 August raced immediately toward Falaise, the entire German Seventh Army would have been caught counter-attacking west toward Mortain, unable to avoid the calamity of a storm-tight encirclement.

J.A. English
Lt-Col, Princess Patricia's Canadian Light Infantry
Professor of Strategy, US Naval War College

PART TWO

HISTORY

CHAPTER I

THE BACKGROUND TO 'TOTALIZE'

During 8–15 August 1944, Lt-Gen Guy G. Simonds' II Canadian Corps launched two set-piece offensives south toward the key high ground located north of Falaise that dominated the vital lateral road that passed through the town. In Operation 'Totalize', fought during 8–10 August, Simonds' forces advanced 15 kilometres (km) south-southeast from the Bourguébus Ridge across a maximum frontage of 13 km. Subsequently, during 14–15 August, Simonds' Operation 'Tractable' – launched from positions north of the Laison River – secured up to a 12-km advance across a maximum frontage of 11 km. (Note that modern maps spell the name of the river both as Laison and Laizon; however, in 1944 the Allied forces invariably used the spelling Laison, so this has been preferred here.) The rapidly changing strategic situation then led Simonds to abandon his stalled Tractable offensive in favour of developing operations on an axis located further to the east. Indeed, by the time Falaise fell on 18 August – a week later than Simonds intended – the strategic situation had so altered that this original objective was by then scarcely significant. II Corps' failure to close the lateral road that ran through Falaise until this date, however, did hamper the development of the wider Allied campaign in Normandy.

To understand the significance of this failure – and thus the significance of these offensives – one must understand how these operations fitted into the overall Normandy campaign. Back on 6 June 1944, the spearhead American, British, and Canadian forces of General Bernard L. Montgomery's 21st Army Group had landed on the Normandy coast. During the following seven weeks fierce German resistance slowed the Allied advance inland, apparently frustrating Montgomery's plan to create a lodgement area bordered by the Loire and Seine Rivers by early September. In contrast, by mid-July the campaign had apparently degenerated into a bloody attritional war of matériel. During late July, however, this attrition began to bear fruit when Lieutenant General Omar N. Bradley's First US Army initiated Operation 'Cobra', its breakthrough offensive against the German Seventh Army front at St-Lô. During 25–26 June – as described in 'Battle Zone Normandy' *Operation Cobra* – this attack successfully broke into the German defensive zone. This initial success owed much to Bradley's use of strategic bombers and massed firepower concentrated on a narrow front, as well as the modest German resistance encountered. The latter resulted from the degradation of German logistic capabilities caused by the previous seven weeks of intense combat, including Montgomery's 18 July 'Goodwood' offensive. Although abortive, this attack – described in 'Battle Zone Normandy' *Battle for Caen* – moved the Anglo-Canadian front forward to the Bourguébus Ridge, from where Simonds subsequently launched Totalize.

Above: II Canadian Corps commander Lt-Gen Guy G. Simonds (*left*) stands up in his scout car to watch Grenadier Guards of Canada Shermans cross the River Seine at Elbeuf on 28 August 1944. *(NAC PA-116585)*

Page 13: At 1130 hours on 14 August, Fort Garry Horse Shermans, supported by flail tanks like the one in the foreground, kick up dust as they redeploy along a small gully, which is identifiable on modern maps as the 90-metre contour line located north-east of la Croix. *(NAC PA-113659)*

Panther tanks such as this contributed to the long-range tank-killing capabilities of the I SS Corps. Here, Mont-Royal Fusiliers inspect a knocked-out *Hitlerjugend* Panther near St André on 9 August. The vehicle's tactical number (132) shows it is the second vehicle in the third troop of the 1st Company (and thus the 1st Battalion) of 12th SS Panzer Regiment. *(NAC PA-114369)*

During 27–28 July, ruthless American exploitation south beyond Coutances transformed the initial success of Cobra into the first potentially decisive Allied breakthrough achieved in Normandy. To widen this rupture, on 30 July Lieutenant-General (Lt-Gen) Miles C. Dempsey's Second (British) Army launched Operation 'Bluecoat', an improvised offensive that aimed to secure Vire and Vassy. Meanwhile, American forces boldly thrust south to secure critical bridgeheads over the Sée and Sélune Rivers beyond Avranches and Pontabault on 31 July. With the German front now torn wide open, and with American forces having turned the bottom corner of the Cotentin peninsula, the Americans could then break out west into Brittany, south toward the Loire, and east toward the Seine. During 1–6 August, American forces burst out in all directions into the interior of France, aided by the daring mobile warfare operations executed by Lt Gen George S. Patton's newly-deployed Third US Army.

The arrival of this second American army in theatre led to the creation of the 12th US Army Group led by former First Army commander Bradley.

On 2 August, Hitler made the gravest strategic error of the entire campaign, a decision that sealed the fate of the German Army in the West. He ordered the new commander of Army Group B, *Generalfeldmarschall* (Field Marshal) Günther Hans von Kluge, to launch a strategic counter-offensive. This riposte aimed to punch through to the Cotentin coast at Avranches, thus encircling all the American divisions that had broken out from Normandy, which could then be annihilated in a 'cauldron battle' in the classic German style. Hitler's plan sought the highest possible return – not just the stabilisation of the ruptured Normandy front line, but a significant strategic success that might alter the entire course of the war in the West. By striving for objectives far beyond the by-then modest capabilities of the German Army in the West, Hitler condemned it to destruction.

During 2–5 August, the German command hastily amassed around Mortain the elements of six weak mechanised divisions under the command of *General der Panzertruppen* (General of Armoured Troops) Hans von Funck's XLVII Panzer Corps, and even managed to assemble sufficient supplies for a few days of offensive action. The Germans only achieved this, however, by denuding the rest of the front of desperately needed reinforcements and supplies, which consequently yielded to continuing Allied attacks. During the night of 6/7 August, in Operation 'Lüttich', von Funck's force attacked west toward Mortain and Avranches along the narrow corridor that ran between the Rivers Sée and Sélune. Initially, the German forces gained some ground, reaching Mortain, but the unyielding American defence of Hill 317 disrupted the development of the attack. During 7 August, moreover, American reinforcements arrived in the area and the skies cleared, allowing Allied fighter-bombers to wreak havoc among the German columns. Within 48 hours, Lüttich – in any case an over-ambitious scheme with little prospect of success – had been driven back beyond its original starting positions.

The strategic significance of Lüttich was that it pushed German forces to the west, deeper into an encirclement that was forming in the Mortain–Argentan area. For, by 8 August when Totalize began, Patton's Third Army – in addition to clearing much of Brittany and approaching the River Loire near Nantes – had outflanked von Funck's forces by advancing 100 km south-east from St-Hilaire-du-Harcouët to take le Mans. Meanwhile, the German front facing Montgomery's Anglo-Canadian armies remained relatively static, stretching from the coast west of the Dives across the Bourguébus Ridge to Aunay-sur-Odon, Mont Pinçon and finally Vire, where the First US Army sector began. By 8 August, therefore, it now seemed increasingly possible that the Allies could in the near future encircle – and subsequently annihilate – an entire German army in a pocket, closed either in the Argentan–Falaise area (the so-called 'small envelopment', which the Americans advocated), or else along the River Seine (the 'large envelopment', which Montgomery preferred).

On 7 August 1944 at the First Canadian Army's Amblie Headquarters, General Crerar (behind the desk) briefed war correspondents regarding the forthcoming Totalize offensive. Visible on the left-hand map board are what appear to be the various phase lines of the intended attack. *(NAC PA-128284)*

It was in this context that Simonds' II Canadian Corps undertook Operations Totalize and Tractable. Given that the Americans were then storming through the interior of France while Montgomery's Anglo-Canadian forces remained bottled up in the dense Norman countryside, it became politically crucial that the latter now contributed significantly to the seemingly looming German defeat. If Simonds' corps could advance south from the Bourguébus Ridge to Falaise, it could cut the key lateral road that ran west from Condé to that town. As Totalize unfolded during 8–10 August, it became increasingly possible that, in so doing, Simonds' forces might prevent the German Seventh Army from withdrawing east out of its looming encirclement. If Simonds' forces achieved this, they might subsequently be able to strike south-south-east to seal any pocket that had formed by linking up with the northward advance of Patton's spearheads.

The experience derived from Operation 'Spring', however, suggested that at any attack launched from the Bourguébus Ridge toward Falaise would meet tough opposition. For, during 25–26 July, Simonds' corps attempted to seize dominating high ground that would facilitate any subsequent offensive across the Falaise plain. In the initial phases of Operation Spring, 2nd and 3rd Canadian Infantry Divisions were to assault the well-prepared German forward defensive localities (FDLs) of May-sur-Orne, Fontenay-le-Marmion, Verrières, Rocquancourt, and Tilly-la-Campagne. In subsequent phases, armoured forces would push south to seize the Verrières Ridge and Hill 122 (the modern Point 118). Unfortunately, Operation Spring was a costly failure that gained no significant ground, largely because the rather unimpressively executed Canadian operation had attacked powerful German defensive positions that were manned in part by determined SS troops.

After this setback, Simonds concluded that any repeat offensive launched from the Bourguébus Ridge would need to be carefully planned and then firmly 'gripped' during its execution if it was to stand any chance of success. Such planning soon began, for on 30 July Montgomery told Simonds to get ready to launch an offensive toward Falaise in about 10 days time, depending on how the advance of Bradley's forces altered the strategic situation. Humiliated by the failure of Spring, Simonds seized this opportunity to redeem his military reputation. Consequently, on 1 August – by which time the II Canadian Corps had come under the command of Lt-Gen Henry D.G. Crerar's newly operational First Canadian Army – Simonds produced an appreciation of the mission that Montgomery had allocated him.

In this insightful document, Simonds concluded that an attack toward Falaise could still achieve success despite the fierce German resistance it would meet. Such resistance would arise because the Germans had deployed in this sector – which they viewed as the key 'hinge' that supported their forces located further west – elements of the fanatical 1st and 12th SS Panzer Divisions *Leibstandarte* and *Hitlerjugend*. Simonds' appreciation recognised that any future planning would have to address three key factors if such an offensive was to secure success. First, this planning had to reflect the German defensive system, which comprised a forward line that ran east from May-sur-Orne through to la Hogue, and about 7.5 km further south a partially prepared reserve position between Bretteville-sur-Laize and St-Sylvain. Simonds concluded that this defensive system compelled the Allies to mount two separate break-in battles.

One of the nine operational Panthers fielded by the *Hitlerjugend* Division's Battlegroup *Wünsche* on 8 August. Over the ensuing week, Panthers returning from short-term repair seem to have more than compensated for vehicles lost in combat. Here, Mont-Royal Fusiliers inspect a knocked-out Panther near St-André on 9 August, while their comrades operate a field radio. (*NAC PA-169293*)

This planning also needed to ensure that, unlike previous Allied operations in Normandy, the attack's forward momentum did not falter just as it reached the depths of the German defensive zone. If Simonds employed all available air support to assist the initial break-in battle, the only fire support left available for the second break-in would be the few artillery pieces that had managed to move forward. Thus, Simonds decided to support the initial break-in with just half of his available air power; to compensate for this, his forces would execute a daring night assault, backed by all available artillery pieces, to penetrate the initial German defences speedily. This method would enable the Allies to keep back half their aerial resources – their day bombers – to support the second break-in battle, which would be mounted just as Allied artillery support declined. Simonds concluded that this approach would ensure that the offensive swiftly penetrated the entire depth of the German defences, thus permitting rapid exploitation toward Falaise.

Second, Simonds' appreciation also asserted that any plan would have to accept that the terrain favoured the defenders. The ground was open and dominated by German-controlled high ground such as Hill 122, and thus Allied forces would enjoy little protection from the long-range killing power of well-concealed tanks and anti-tank guns. To obtain success, therefore, any attack toward Falaise had to minimise these defensive capabilities. To do this, Simonds argued, any Allied offensive would have to be made when German observation was handicapped, preferably by darkness. Any such operation, of course, would also have to take steps to minimise the command and control problems that would arise during a night advance. Simonds also concluded that a night assault was appropriate because, as any future operation toward Falaise could not secure tactical surprise in terms of objectives or the axis of attack since these remained obvious, it therefore needed to achieve surprise in terms of method and timing.

Third, Simonds also recognised that his intended offensive would have to destroy – rather than just suppress – the deep German anti-tank positions. Consequently, he decided to use night infiltration tactics, in which all-arms mobile columns would by-pass the forward defences and race through the depth of the initial German position. These columns would generate momentum, disrupt the initial defensive zone throughout its depth, overrun anti-tank and artillery positions, and secure key high ground. Simonds also argued that the infantry in the columns would have to be embussed in armoured vehicles so that they could keep up with the armour, and once on the objective help the latter repel German counter-strikes. Finally, Simonds' appreciation indicated the forces his corps required to execute this mission successfully. In addition to all available artillery and aerial support, II Corps required three infantry divisions (backed by two independent armoured brigades), two armoured divisions, a searchlight battery for night illumination, and Crocodile flame-throwing tanks for night consolidation tasks.

At 1100 hours on 5 August, Lt-Gen Crerar held a briefing on the forthcoming offensive – now called Totalize – during which he stressed that, as the campaign had reached 'a potentially decisive period', a successful operation might lead to 'a quick termination of the war'. Crerar also observed that Totalize would commence on the same date – 8 August – as had the Amiens offensive in 1918, a day that had been the German Army's 'black day'. Crerar now hoped that Totalize would make 8 August 1944 an even blacker day for the Germans than it had been 26 years previously. The briefing culminated at noon when Simonds' outlined his original corps plan for Totalize to the assembled officers. This plan envisaged that, after strategic night bombers had struck targets on the flanks of the attack, two infantry divisions would execute the initial night break-in operation. Then, a little after noon the next day, a second strategic bombing run would hit the reserve German defensive position. Subsequently, in the offensive's second phase, an armoured division would then break through this second line, before two armoured divisions advanced 14 km south-southeast during the final phase to seize the key high ground situated north of Falaise.

Army commander Lt-Gen H.D.G. Crerar (*left*), 2nd Canadian Infantry Division commander Maj-Gen Charles Foulkes (*centre*), and (*right*) Lt-Gen Guy G. Simonds – attend a memorial service at Dieppe in September 1944 for the soldiers lost there in 1942. (*NAC PA-116584*)

On 6 August, however, battlefield events overtook this plan after the Allies learned that the *Leibstandarte* had withdrawn from the initial German defensive line. Allied intelligence erroneously assumed that this formation had redeployed to bolster the second German position, whereas in reality it was *en route* to another part of the front. Simonds now concluded that his planned initial break-in might prove easier – and the second break-in more difficult – than he had anticipated, and so at noon that day he issued a modified corps plan. Given the perceived

Priest carriers transport 1st Black Watch infantrymen forward to the left British column's initial assembly area at Cormelles during the evening of 7 August. These are some of the 60 surplus Priest self-propelled guns that Simonds had converted into armoured personnel carriers. *(The Tank Museum, Bovington [TTM] 2292/E6)*

bolstering of the second German line, Simonds' new scheme now committed two entire armoured divisions simultaneously to the second break-in across a significantly widened frontage. His new concept also amalgamated the operation's original second and third phases into a new consolidated second phase, this change being designed to drive the Allied armour forward so that it secured the high ground north of Falaise by 9 August. In so doing, Simonds also hoped to exploit any tactical advantage that would accrue to the Allies in the immediate aftermath of the second bombing run. Finally, while the tasks Simonds' new plan set his infantry divisions during the initial break-in remained unchanged, he now allocated them markedly more ambitious missions during the second break-in.

To implement this plan, by 7 August 1944 Simonds had amassed 85,000 front-line troops backed by 2,000 aircraft and 720 artillery pieces. His concept of operations envisaged that, from 2300 hours on 7 August, two infantry divisions would execute the initial night break-in operation (Phase I). On the

Then: A mixed column of Canadian vehicles heads north past the badly-damaged church in Rocquancourt on 11 August 1944. *(NAC PA-190014)*

Now: The damage done to Rocquancourt church in 1944 has long since been repaired. Sadly, the recent addition of the bus shelter represents an all-too-typical example of contemporary Norman architecture. (Author)

Allied right (the western sector), Major-General (Maj-Gen) Charles Foulkes' 2nd Canadian Infantry Division was to attack with 2nd Canadian Armoured Brigade under command (*see box opposite*). On the sector east of the main Caen–Falaise road (the modern N158), the British 51st (Highland) Division was to operate with the British 33rd Armoured Brigade under command (*see box, p. 26*). The three lead infantry battalions of each of these divisions, whose soldiers would be embussed in armoured vehicles, would link up with armoured forces and other supporting arms to form three Canadian and three British mobile columns; a seventh column was formed from the 2nd Canadian Division's reconnaissance regiment. These columns would spearhead the initial night break-in operation by rapidly infiltrating between the German FDLs to seize key objectives up to 6.3 km behind the front line.

Order of Battle: 2nd Canadian Infantry Division 7 August 1944

Commander:	*Maj-Gen Charles Foulkes*
4th Canadian Infantry Brigade	*Brig F.N. Ganong*
The Royal Regiment of Canada	
The Royal Hamilton Light Infantry	
The Essex Scottish	
5th Canadian Infantry Brigade	*Brig W.J. Megill*
The Black Watch of Canada	
Le Régiment de Maisonneuve	
The Calgary Highlanders	
6th Canadian Infantry Brigade	*Brig H.A. Young*
Les Fusiliers Mont-Royal	
The Cameron Highlanders of Canada	
The South Saskatchewan Regiment	

Divisional units:
8th Reconnaissance Regiment (14th Canadian Hussars)
The Toronto Scottish Regiment
2nd Anti-Tank Regiment, RCA
4th, 5th, 6th Field Regiments, RCA

Plus under command:	
2nd Canadian Armoured Brigade	*Brig R.A. Wyman*
6th Canadian Armoured Regiment (1st Hussars)	
10th Canadian Armoured Regiment (Fort Garry Horse)	
27th Canadian Armoured Regiment (Sherbrooke Fusiliers)	

1st Lothian and Border Yeomanry [British, from 30th Armd Bde]

In this first phase, the 2nd Canadian Division's four columns were to secure Caillouet, Gaumesnil, the quarry between these hamlets, and Hill 122. These objectives represented key high ground, major communications nodes, artillery or anti-tank gun areas, or some combination of these characteristics. As the Canadian mobile column assault unfolded during that night, the three infantry battalions of 6th Canadian Brigade were simultaneously to advance on foot. Their missions were to secure the villages of May-sur-Orne, Fontenay-le-Marmion, and Rocquancourt, which the advancing columns would have by-passed. From dawn on 8 August, after the 2nd Division had secured these seven objectives, it was to establish a firm base within this 6.3-km deep and 5-km wide penetration of the German lines. Subsequently, during the morning, 4th Canadian Armoured Division would pass through this firm base in readiness to initiate the offensive's second phase.

Order of Battle: 51st (Highland) Division
7 August 1944

Commander:	*Maj-Gen T.G. Rennie*
152nd Infantry Brigade	*Brig A.J.H. Cassels*

2nd Battalion, The Seaforth Highlanders
5th Battalion, The Seaforth Highlanders
5th Battalion, The Cameron Highlanders

153rd Infantry Brigade — *Brig H. Murray*

5th Battalion, The Black Watch
1st Battalion, The Gordon Highlanders
5th/7th Battalion, The Gordon Highlanders

154th Infantry Brigade — *Brig J.A. Oliver*

1st Battalion, The Black Watch
7th Battalion, The Black Watch
7th Battalion, The Argyll & Sutherland Highlanders

Divisional units:

2nd Derbyshire Yeomanry
1st/7th Battalion, The Middlesex Regiment
6th Anti-Tank Regiment, RA
126th, 127th, 128th Field Regiments, RA

Plus under command:

33rd Armoured Brigade — *Brig H.B. Scott*

144th Regiment, RAC
148th Regiment, RAC
1st Northamptonshire Yeomanry

Meanwhile, 51st (Highland) Division was to carry out the initial break-in operation east of the main Caen–Falaise road. Spearheading this mission were three mobile columns, each of which combined an armoured regiment, an embussed infantry battalion and supporting arms to form a force of around 1,900 men with up to 200 vehicles. The right forward column was to advance 5.3 km south-southeast to capture Cramesnil, the right rear column was to advance 3.8 km south-east to take Garcelles-Secqueville, while the left column – deployed 1.5 km east of the other two formations – was to advance 6.3 km south-southeast to capture St-Aignan-de-Cramesnil. Subsequently, during the afternoon of 8 August, the 1st Gordon Highlanders – part of the division's 153rd Brigade – were to march 2.4 km south-east from Bourguébus to secure Secqueville and the woods to the east, thus providing flank protection for the left column.

Allied Deployment for Totalize – Phase I
7 August 1944

Unit (mode of operation)	Deployed
Western (Canadian) Sector – 2nd Canadian Infantry Division	
Fusiliers Mont-Royal (on foot)	St-André
Camerons of Canada (on foot)	W of Beauvoir Farm
Essex Scottish, Sherbrooke Fusiliers, Fort Garry Horse (in column)	W of Beauvoir Farm
Royal Hamiltons, Sherbrooke Fusiliers, Fort Garry Horse (in column)	W of Beauvoir Farm
Royal Regiment, Sherbrooke Fusiliers, Fort Garry Horse (in column)	W of Beauvoir Farm
Black Watch of Canada (on foot)	Beauvoir–Troteval Farms*
Régiment de Maisonneuve (on foot)	Beauvoir–Troteval Farms*
Calgary Highlanders (on foot)	Beauvoir–Troteval Farms*
South Saskatchewans (on foot)	Troteval Farm
14th Hussars, Fort Garry Horse (in column)	E of Troteval Farm
Eastern (British) Sector – 51st (Highland) Division	
5th Camerons (on foot)	E of la Guingette
7th Argylls, 144th RAC (in column)	E of la Guingette
7th Black Watch, 148th RAC (in column)	E of la Guingette
2nd Seaforths (on foot)	W of Hubert-Folie
5th Seaforths (on foot)	W of Hubert-Folie*
1st Black Watch, 1st Northants Yeomanry (in column)	Hubert-Folie–Soliers
5th Black Watch (on foot)	Bourguébus–Soliers*
1st Gordons (on foot)	Bourguébus–Soliers*
5th/7th Gordons (on foot)	Bourguébus–Soliers*

reserve units

As the British columns advanced deep into the initial German defences, two marching infantry battalions from 152nd Brigade were simultaneously to capture the German FDLs that these columns had by-passed. The 2nd Seaforth Highlanders were to march south between the axes of advance developed by the right and left British columns to seize Tilly-la-Campagne. Meanwhile, the 5th Cameron Highlanders were to march behind the two right columns to secure Lorguichon and the nearby woods, while the brigade's final battalion – the 5th Seaforth Highlanders – remained in reserve. These foot missions were just as important as the more dramatic column assaults. If these by-passed FDLs continued to hold out, their fire could interdict the forward movement of Allied forces and supplies up the nearby axes of advance cleared by the columns, and thus slow the offensive's momentum. Maj-Gen Rennie understandably assumed that once the columns had outflanked these positions, the morale of their garrisons would collapse; consequently, he did not anticipate that the foot infantry would encounter fierce resistance and so did not provide them with tank support. By 0800 hours on 8 August, therefore, Rennie expected that his three columns and two marching battalions would have secured their objectives and established a firm base within this 6.3-km deep, 2.4-km wide, penetration of the German front.

To support this initial break-in Simonds aimed to employ, in addition to night strategic bombers, all his available 720 artillery pieces. To preserve surprise, Simonds eschewed any preliminary artillery bombardment prior to the start of the operation, which instead commenced with Royal Air Force (RAF) strategic bombers striking seven targets to protect the offensive's flanks from enfilade fire. Hence, once the ground forces had commenced their assault, they had to rely solely on the suppressive effect inflicted by either this aerial bombing or a creeping artillery barrage. At 2345 hours on 7 August, 340 artillery pieces were to lay down this barrage across a 4-km front located 1.5 km south of the corps' start line – the road that ran east from St-André-sur-Orne to Soliers. These guns would gradually extend their fire south so that the barrage moved forward at a rate of 200 metres every two minutes to an eventual depth of 6 km. In addition, the corps' 380 remaining guns were to deliver counter-battery fire against every identified or suspected German artillery, rocket-launcher or mortar position.

Simonds slated the second phase of Totalize to commence at 1400 hours on 8 August, after US Army Air Force (USAAF) strategic day bombers had struck six targets located along the second German defensive position. Subsequently, Allied fighter-bombers were to attack targets further south, including Grainville-Langannerie, Urville, Estrées-la-Campagne, and Quesnay wood. Once the strategic air strikes had ended, the 4th

Canadian and 1st Polish Armoured Divisions were to pass through the vanguard infantry divisions and strike south. The 4th Division was to advance down (and to the west of) the main Caen–Falaise road, break through the second German defence line around Haut Mesnil – which it was hoped would still be disrupted after the bombing – and then secure the high ground north-west of Bretteville-le-Rabet. Simultaneously, to the east of the main road, the Polish Division would thrust south from St-Aignan to rupture the second German line around Cauvicourt.

Allied Artillery used in Totalize

Unit	Equipment
2nd Canadian Infantry Division Field Artillery	72 x towed 25-pdr
3rd Canadian Infantry Division Field Artillery	48 x towed 25-pdr
51st (Highland) Division Field Artillery	72 x towed 25-pdr
4th Canadian Armoured Division Field Artillery	24 x towed 25-pdr
	24 x self-propelled 25-pdr
(+19th Field Regiment, RCA)	24 x 105-mm
1st Polish Armoured Division Field Artillery	24 x towed 25-pdr
	24 x self-propelled 25-pdr
Attached artillery of 49th Infantry Division	72 x towed 25-pdr
Total field artillery	*384*
2nd Army Group Royal Canadian Artillery	64 x 5.5-inch
	8 x 7.2-inch
	8 x 155-mm.
3rd Army Group Royal Artillery	64 x 5.5-inch
	8 x 7.2-inch
	8 x 155-mm
4th Army Group Royal Artillery	64 x 5.5-inch
	8 x 7.2-inch
	8 x 155-mm
9th Army Group Royal Artillery	48 x 5.5-inch
Total medium/heavy artillery	*288*
2nd Canadian Heavy Anti-Aircraft Regiment	24 x 3.7-inch
109th Heavy Anti-Aircraft Regiment	24 x 3.7-inch
Total heavy anti-aircraft artillery	*48*
Total artillery	**720**
Ammunition dumped forward:	200,000 shells

600 rounds per gun (field: 25-pdr, 105-mm),
300 rpg (medium: 5.5-in, 155-mm), & 100 rpg (heavy: 7.2-in)

Source: II Canadian Corps Operational Order No. 5, 7 August 1944, Appendix B.

Having penetrated this second German position, Simonds expected his armour to generate offensive momentum that afternoon. Once beyond Bretteville-le-Rabet, 4th Division was to swing south-west to capture the key ridge situated in the la Fontaine–Fontaine-le-Pin area. Meanwhile, the Poles were to advance south-east from Cauvicourt to secure Hills 184 and 159 (the modern Points 183 and 161). To assist this advance, each armoured division could call down pre-arranged artillery concentrations delivered by its organic field artillery and an allocated Army Group Royal Artillery (AGRA). While these armoured thrusts unfolded, Simonds' infantry divisions were also to mount subsidiary operations. The 3rd Canadian Division was to secure the western flank by capturing Bretteville-sur-Laize, 51st (Highland) Division was to consolidate the eastern flank by seizing the woods south-east of Robert Mesnil, while 2nd Canadian Division was to maintain its firm base in the St-André–Gaumesnil area. Finally, the 3rd Canadian Division was then to move forward and consolidate the area located between Haut Mesnil and Hill 140 (the modern Point 138) once the armour had advanced south beyond this area.

1st Polish Armoured Division soldiers take some sustenance in a field near Caen on 7 August, the day before their first action. (NAC PA-115782)

Simonds had based this final Totalize plan on his understanding of how the German forces that faced him were deployed. During early August, the élite I SS Panzer Corps – part of *General der Panzertruppen* Eberbach's Fifth Panzer Army –

manned the Bourguébus Ridge sector of the Normandy front. On 7 August, the 89th Infantry Division manned the right-hand segment of the corps' front that ran east from the River Orne north-west of May-sur-Orne through to la Hogue, where it linked up with the sector controlled by the neighbouring LXXXVI Corps. The 1056th Grenadier Regiment held the division's western sector (from May through to Verrières), while the 1055th Regiment defended the eastern sector; both units deployed two battalions forward and one in reserve. These four forward battalions had established their main defensive positions in May, Fontenay, Verrières, Rocquancourt, Tilly, and la Hogue, as well as along the Verrières Ridge.

German Artillery Dispositions
8 August 1944

Artillery   *(approx. 120 guns in all)*
    189th Artillery Regiment (89th Division)
    12th SS Panzer Artillery Regiment (12th SS Division)
    271st Artillery Regiment (271st Division)
    2 x Army Heavy Artillery Battalions (corps troops)
The above were deployed at 9 locations:
    Fontenay-le-Marmion, defile west of Caillouet, wood north-east of
    Bretteville-sur-Laize, Cintheaux, orchards near St-Aignan-de-Cramesnil,
    Bretteville-le-Rabet, Robert Mesnil, Secqueville, St-Sylvain

Rocket Launchers
    1 x Independent Nebelwerfer Regiment   *(establishment 54 Nebelwerfers)*
Deployed at six locations:
    West of River Laize opposite Fontenay, west of River Laize opposite
    Caillouet, in Caillouet (at least one launcher), in Haut Mesnil quarry,
    near Cramesnil, in woods near Secqueville

Mortars
    78 x divisional mortars (89th & 12th SS Divisions)

To support the infantrymen, who had dug in behind the many thick hedges found in this area, both regiments had deployed numerous machine guns and mortars well forward, together with two batteries of divisional artillery and a corps-level self-propelled anti-tank gun battery. The two reserve battalions had deployed further back around Caillouet and St-Aignan, ready to mount a riposte against any Allied penetration of the line. The division had also deployed most of its organic artillery regiment and anti-tank battalion, plus an attached corps self-propelled anti-tank unit, to depth positions that stretched from Caillouet through Cintheaux to St-Aignan.

Order of Battle: 12th SS Panzer Division
8 August 1944

Commander: *SS-Oberführer Kurt Meyer*

Battlegroup *Waldmüller*   *SS-Sturmbannführer Hans Waldmüller*
    1st Company, 12th SS Anti-Tank Bn   *(20 Panzerjäger IV tank destroyers)*
    1st Battalion, 25th SS Panzergrenadier Regiment   *(c. 600 infantry)*
    101st SS Escort Company (corps troops)   *(c. 100 infantry)*

Battlegroup *Wünsche*   *SS-Obersturmbannführer Max Wünsche*
    Elements 12th SS Panzer Regiment   *(37 Panzer IVs and 9 Panthers)*
    2nd Company, 101st SS Heavy Tank Battalion   *(8 Tigers, corps troops)*
                  SS-Hauptsturmführer Michael Wittmann)
(NB: Elements of this command were often subordinated to BG *Waldmüller*)

Battlegroup *Krause*   *SS-Sturmbannführer Bernhard Krause*
    Parts 1st and 3rd Bns, 26th SS Panzergrenadier Regt   *(c. 1,000 infantry)*
(NB: initially deployed west of Laize)

Other forces:
    12th SS Escort Company   *(c. 100 infantry)*
    Reconnaissance Group *Wienecke*
    12th SS Anti-Aircraft Battalion
    12th SS Mortar Battalion
    12th SS Artillery Regiment (bulk of)

    Total: ***4,500 personnel***
             (including 1,800 infantry), 74 AFVs

(NB: These groupings were regularly changed.)

Allied intelligence did not expect the 89th Division to offer resolute resistance to Totalize. The Germans had only raised this reduced-establishment formation from low-category personnel during 1944, and it had not seen combat prior to reaching Normandy. Moreover, two other divisions of the same wave – the 77th and 91st – had not displayed marked defensive resilience in the earlier Normandy battles. The I SS Corps apparently also shared this assessment, since its defence plan envisaged that, when a successful Allied attack had rendered the initial front untenable, the 89th Division would withdraw back to the second defence line. Therefore, while it was this formation that would initially bear the brunt of resisting Totalize, the brigade-sized *Hitlerjugend* battlegroup deployed as corps reserve constituted the corps' principal defensive asset. Divisional commander

SS-Oberführer (Brigadier) Kurt Meyer had deployed his units either in the Laison Valley or else west of the River Laize. On 7 August, this formidable fighting force fielded 4,500 well-motivated personnel and some 74 armoured fighting vehicles. Meyer deployed his men in a series of loosely organised tactical battlegroups (*see opposite*).

Elements of two other German formations, also played marginal roles in halting Totalize. On the western flank, units of the 271st Infantry Division engaged Simonds' forces along the River Laize, while on the eastern flank elements of the 272nd Infantry Division – part of the neighbouring LXXXVI Corps – defended Secqueville against the British attacks mounted during the afternoon of 8 August.

German prisoners, probably including some from the 271st Infantry Division, march through Fleury-sur-Orne on 9 August 1944. *(NAC PA-169322)*

The corps' defensive capabilities were also augmented by the presence in the area of a brigade from the *Luftwaffe*'s III Flak Corps. This formation had deployed its 65 dual-purpose 88-mm flak/anti-tank guns along the second defensive position and further south around Potigny. According to Meyer, however, as Totalize unfolded the *Luftwaffe* did not subordinate these units to his command, and so most of these guns apparently continued to protect vulnerable points located further south from air attack rather than being used as anti-tank weapons to bolster the crumbling German defence. Significant indirect fire assets, moreover, also augmented the corps' defensive combat power. These included 78 divisional mortars, a *Nebelwerfer* rocket-launcher regiment and, in addition to the divisional artillery, two independent heavy artillery battalions (*see box, p. 31*).

CHAPTER 2

THE BREAK-IN PHASE OF 'TOTALIZE'

From 2300 hours on 7 August, 1,020 RAF strategic bombers began to bomb seven targets on the offensive's flanks, which had been marked by artillery-delivered coloured flares. The dust thrown up by the first strikes, however, so obscured the battle-field that many subsequent aircraft, for safety reasons, did not bomb because they had not definitely identified their targets and so no more than 3,462 tonnes of munitions were delivered. As the Allies had anticipated, this night operation encountered only modest anti-aircraft fire; just ten planes failed to return. Then, from 2330 hours, after the bombing had ended, the seven Allied mobile columns and the five foot-infantry battalions crossed their respective start lines along a 5.8-km front. Each column had formed up in a dense formation, with each row four vehicles abreast on a 16-metre front and with up to 50 rows extending back 400 metres. The Allied command was aware that the problems these columns faced in maintaining their direction and cohesion in the darkness were more likely to hinder their advance than German resistance. For Totalize, therefore, they had instituted various special measures to ameliorate these problems.

Allied Special Command and Control Measures

Each column's lead vehicle had its position and the bearing of its thrust line fixed by survey

Signals units projected four radio beams along the main axes of advance

Searchlights projected diffused illumination above the columns

Bofors guns fired tracer along the columns' axes of advance

Artillery fired green marker shells onto Hill 122 (when bombing had ended)

HISTORY

The 400-metre deep, 150-metre wide Canadian triple column formation assembled in the left-hand part of these fields. This view, taken from the D89 road some 200 metres east of the intersection with the D235, looks north toward the villages of Ifs (800 metres distant in the centre) and Bras (right). *(Author)*

At 2330 hours, the four Canadian columns began to advance south-southeast at 11 km/hr from the road that ran east from St-André to la Guinguette. Three of these columns had formed up in close proximity some 100 metres west of Beauvoir Farm. They were separated by 50 metre gaps, across a total frontage of 150 metres. In each of these three columns an embussed infantry battalion had married up with one or two squadrons of tanks, plus supporting arms such as towed anti-tank guns, machine-gun carriers and flail mine-clearing tanks. These columns' infantry components came from the 4th Canadian Brigade, the flails from the British 1st Lothian and Border Yeomanry, and the tanks from the 10th Canadian Armoured Regiment (the Fort Garry Horse) or the 27th Canadian Armoured Regiment (the Sherbrooke Fusiliers). The Essex Scottish column deployed on the western axis of this triple-column formation, while along the central axis came the Royal Regiment of Canada column, and to the east that of the Royal Hamilton Light Infantry. The western column was to capture Caillouet, the central column Hill 122, and the eastern column Gaumesnil and the nearby quarry. The dramatic events experienced by these three columns during the night 7–8 August will not be described here, since they are examined in Tour A, Stands A1 and A2 (see pp. 119–29).

View taken from Point 62 (470 metres south of Troteval Farm) looking east across the fields of le Clos de la Vigne toward the small copse at le Noyer, 1,000 metres away by the N158. The 14th Hussars column advanced south-southeast (from left to right) across this area on an axis 450 metres east of (and parallel with) the main Caen–Falaise road until it had passed east of Rocquancourt. *(Author)*

The fourth Canadian column – based around Lt-Col B.M. Always' 8th Reconnaissance Regiment (the 14th Hussars) and two troops of Fort Garry Horse Shermans – also crossed its start line at 2330 hours. This column had formed up east of Troteval Farm on the St-André–la Guinguette road, 1,200 metres east of the triple-column formation. The column's 200 vehicles were to advance south-southeast for 4.3 km until they were opposite Hill 122, where they would swing east-southeast across the main road and then assault the north-west corner of this high ground.

As the leading vehicles of this force, as well as those in the other three Canadian columns, rumbled south through the darkness, they used the searchlights, the Bofors tracer, and the wireless beams projected over their heads to navigate themselves toward their objectives. The vehicles in the subsequent rows, meanwhile, navigated themselves simply by following the tail-lights of the vehicles that immediately preceded them. At 2345 hours, the artillery began to lay down the creeping barrage, which all four columns then followed as it progressed south at 6 km/hr through the German lines. Soon, the passage of 800 vehicles across the sun-baked earth generated dense dust clouds that, when combined with the thick smoke created by the barrage, reduced the already poor night-time visibility to just a few metres. In this all-pervasive gloom, many vehicles lost their direction and inadvertently veered away from the columns, causing the dense formations to disintegrate. Soon the Germans adopted the clever tactic of seeking to exacerbate the confusion already being experienced within the columns by firing artillery smoke rounds into the dust-thickened darkness.

With growing desperation, the columns repeatedly radioed higher command, imploring them to increase the intensity of the searchlight beams directed above their heads, but even these augmented beams failed to provide much illumination through the ever-thickening morass of dust and smoke that had engulfed the battlefield. For the first 45 minutes, however, the spearhead vehicles did somehow manage to follow the Bofors tracer streams fired over their heads, but sadly at 0015 hours the gunners ended this navigational aid as planned. After this, the columns found maintaining formation cohesion in the brooding gloom increasingly difficult and consequently their vehicles continued to become scattered across the battlefield. Despite these difficulties, Lt-Col Always' column nevertheless made steady progress south for the first 90 minutes of its advance. The night assault had caught the Germans by surprise, and hence the column initially only encountered disorganised resistance. By 0230 hours the force had advanced 3.5 km to close on the appositely named hamlet of la Guerre, located 700 metres east-southeast of Rocquancourt. Here, however, determined resistance halted the column's advance until dawn, when Always concluded that his force could not now capture Hill 122, judging that, without the advantages of surprise and the darkness, any assault would incur unacceptably severe casualties. Reluctantly, he ordered his column to consolidate the positions it then held around la Guerre.

While the Canadian columns struck south that night, the three marching infantry battalions of Brigadier Young's 6th Canadian Brigade attempted to secure the German FDLs by-passed by the columns. The principal operation mounted by the brigade that night – the attack executed by Les Fusiliers Mont-Royal on May-sur-Orne – is described in Tour B, Stands B1–B3 (see pp. 136–45). Simultaneously, the South Saskatchewan Regiment (SSR) pushed south to consolidate Rocquancourt after the Canadian columns had passed through this village. Finally, from west of Beauvoir Farm, the Cameron Highlanders of Canada marched 3.2 km south to secure the outflanked German FDL at Fontenay-le-Marmion. No creeping barrage preceded the battalion's advance, and instead it had to rely on the disorientation inflicted on the Germans by the aerial bombing of Fontenay. The combination of German fire and minefields, however, slowed the battalion's advance and hence it was only at 0500 hours that it launched its assault on the village. By 0630 hours, the battalion had secured the northern half of the village but subsequently it struggled to secure the southern part in the face of fierce resistance.

By 0830 hours, moreover, the tactical situation in Fontenay had deteriorated. By then the Cameron Highlanders of Canada had suffered severe casualties during repeated attempts to capture the southern part of the village. Subsequently, after accurate German shelling had inflicted grievous casualties amongst the battalion's headquarters personnel, a counter-attack against the unit's rear flank had cut it off from its lines of communication. In response to the battalion's frantic calls for help, Allied artillery fire rained down on the adjacent German positions. Yet, in response to the unit's request for a relief operation, higher command replied that no additional infantry would be available until after the South Saskatchewans had cleared Rocquancourt of enemy forces. Unfortunately for the Cameron Highlanders, this relief effort did not materialise until early that afternoon. The rescue force comprised two South Saskatchewan infantry companies supported by a squadron from the 6th Canadian Armoured Regiment (1st Hussars). This force advanced west from Rocquancourt and struck the German garrison at Fontenay in the flank and rear; simultaneously, the Cameron Highlanders renewed their frontal attack on the southern half of the village. The flanking attack caught the Germans by surprise, and this enabled the Canadians to overcome the last resistance in the village by 1530 hours. Only after the Canadians had collected together all their prisoners did this unexpectedly large haul of 250 captives bring home to the weary Cameron Highlanders that Allied intelligence had woefully underestimated the strength of the enemy forces in Fontenay.

Back at 2330 hours on the 7th, the South Saskatchewans had also begun their thrust south to secure Rocquancourt, 2 km east of Fontenay. During the first hour of their advance, they managed

Fusiliers Mont-Royal soldiers patrol the devastated streets of May-sur-Orne on 9 August. This operation was the main foot attack mounted by the 6th Canadian Infantry Brigade, while another of the 2nd Canadian Division's formations, the 4th Canadian Infantry Brigade, executed the column assault. In typical doctrinal style, the division held back its final formation, 5th Canadian Infantry Brigade, as a reserve. *(NAC PA-132419)*

to follow closely behind the rolling barrage, and hence encountered little resistance. By 0100 hours the South Saskatchewans had reached Rocquancourt – just as the Royal Hamiltons' column rumbled through the village – and subsequently the infantry began to mop up any remaining German troops. Although the South Saskatchewans soon had most of the village under control after incurring only minimal casualties, a few German soldiers continued to offer dogged resistance until well after dawn. Unfortunately, the delays the Saskatchewans experienced in rooting out these die-hards prevented the battalion from striking west to aid the Cameron Highlanders at Fontenay until early that afternoon.

Overall, by noon on 8 August, the Canadian break-in operation in the western sector had secured a most marked

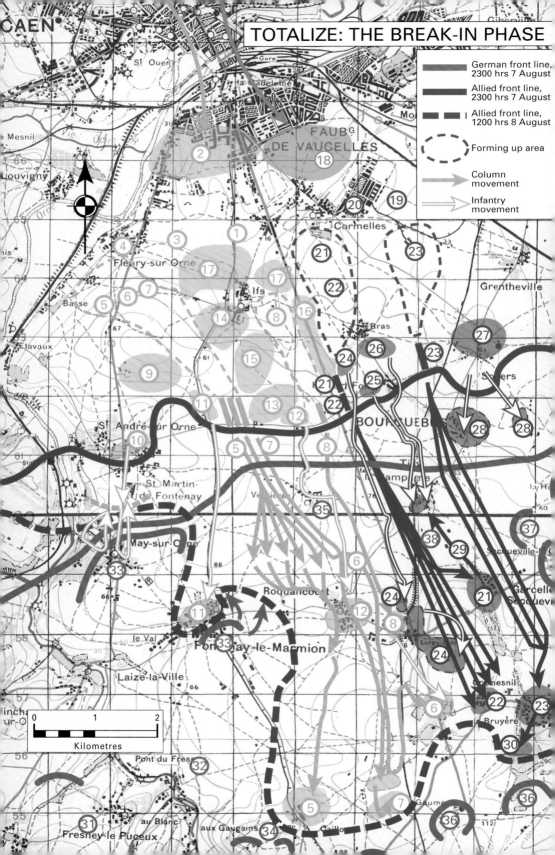

TOTALIZE: THE BREAK-IN PHASE

German front line, 2300 hrs 7 August
Allied front line, 2300 hrs 7 August
Allied front line, 1200 hrs 8 August
Forming up area
Column movement
Infantry movement

CAEN

St Ouen

Mesnil

Louvigny

FAUB^G DE VAUCELLES

Cormelles

Fleury-sur Orne

Grentheville

Baîse

Ifs

Bras

Étavaux

BOURGUEBU

St André-sur Orne

St Martin-de-Fontenay

Verrières

May-sur-O

Roquancourt

le Val

Fontenay-le-Marmion

Laize-la-Ville

Lorguichon

0   1   2
Kilometres

Pont du Fres

inch
ur-O

au Blanc

Fresney-le-Puceux

aux Gaugains

Bruyère

Gaume

(1)	II Canadian Corps sector	(20)	33rd Armoured Brigade sector
(2)	4th Canadian Armoured Division	(21)	British right rear column
(3)	2nd Canadian Infantry Division sector	(22)	British right forward column
(4)	2nd Canadian Armoured Brigade sector	(23)	British left column
(5)	Essex Scottish column	(24)	5th Camerons
(6)	Royal Regiment of Canada column	(25)	2nd Seaforths
(7)	Royal Hamilton Light Infantry column	(26)	5th Seaforths
(8)	14th Hussars column	(27)	153rd Infantry Brigade
(9)	Troop, Fort Garry Horse	(28)	5th Black Watch
(10)	Fusiliers Mont-Royal	(29)	Squadron, 148th RAC
(11)	Camerons of Canada	(30)	A Squadron, 1st Northants Yeomanry
(12)	South Saskatchewan Regiment	(31)	I SS Panzer Corps sector
(13)	Elements 5th Canadian Infantry Brigade	(32)	89th Infantry Division sector
(14)	4th Field Artillery Regiment, RCA	(33)	I/1056th Grenadiers
(15)	5th Field Artillery Regiment, RCA	(34)	II/1056th Grenadiers
(16)	6th Field Artillery Regiment, RCA	(35)	III/1056th Grenadiers
(17)	Artillery elements, RCA	(36)	I/1055th Grenadiers
(18)	1st Polish Armoured Division	(37)	II/1055th Grenadiers
(19)	51st (Highland) Infantry Division sector	(38)	III/1055th Grenadiers
			Base map: GSGS Operation Totalize

success. This achievement validated Simonds' risky decision to use darkness – despite all the problems that inevitably accompanied such an operation – to conceal the Allied advance from the Germans' potent long-range anti-tank assets. Two of the four Canadian columns had secured their objectives, while the remaining two had dug in not far from these locations. In the process, the columns had successfully advanced between 3.6 and 6.3 km to rupture the initial German defence zone. In addition, the marching infantry units had seized one of their three objectives, while at May and Fontenay they were not too far away from doing so. Moreover, while these latter battles had been tougher than Simonds had expected, overall the Canadian advance had encountered only weak resistance, and thus incurred modest casualties amounting to about 160 personnel.

As these Canadian operations unfolded, the British 51st (Highland) Division executed the attacks initiated east of the main road. Three British mobile columns – each comprising one regiment from the 33rd Armoured Brigade, an embussed battalion of Brigadier J.A. Oliver's 154th Infantry Brigade, and

HISTORY

various supporting arms – were to spearhead these operations by penetrating up to 6.3-km deep into the German defences. Deployed 300 metres east of the main Caen–Falaise road, the right forward column fielded the infantry of the 7th Argyll and Sutherland Highlanders, the armour of the 144th Regiment, Royal Armoured Corps (RAC), plus anti-tank guns and flail tanks. Led by Lt-Col A. Jolly of the RAC, this column was to advance south-southeast from la Guinguette to capture Cramesnil, the nearby woods, and the road junction at le Haut Bosq. Assembled behind this was the right rear column, with the infantry of 7th Black Watch and the tanks of 148th RAC. Spearheaded by Captain A.N.J. Nukins' navigator tank, this column was to advance behind Jolly's force for 2.5 km until it had by-passed Tilly-la-Campagne, and then thrust 1.6 km east-southeast to capture Garcelles-Secqueville and the nearby woods. Finally, Lt-Col D. Forster's left column – the infantry of 1st Black Watch, the tanks of 1st Northamptonshire Yeomanry, and some flails – had assembled in fields located 400 metres west-southwest of Soliers. This column was to advance 6.3 km south-southeast, by-passing Garcelles-Secqueville, to capture St-Aignan and the nearby orchards at Delle de la Roque.

A view taken from the western fringes of Soliers looking east along the D89 road. Visible beyond the bridge, in the fields to the right of the road, is the location where Lt-Col Forster's left British column assembled around 2300 hours on 7 August. This shot also depicts the location for Stand A3, on the southern (left) end of the bridge looking left along the embankment toward Bourguébus. *(Author)*

These British columns also assembled in dense formations with up to 50 rows of vehicles deployed on a frontage of four machines, so as to prevent them from disintegrating during their night-time advance. Typically, a navigator's vehicle headed each column, followed by mine-clearing flails, an armoured squadron, then the embussed infantry interspersed with additional tanks, and finally the towed anti-tank guns. These columns assembled south of Cormelles-le-Royal at 2200 hours on 7 August and then moved along illuminated routes to their various start lines. At 2330 hours the right forward and left columns crossed their start lines, with the right rear column following on some 45 minutes later.

The experiences of the left British column are explored in Tour A, Stands A3–A4 (*see pp. 129–34*), so this narrative will focus solely on the actions of the two right British columns.

View from the British right forward column's start line looking south-southeast along its axis of advance across the fields of la Chasse and le Val toward the Lorguichon woods. Initially, the column successfully covered 1.3 km despite the poor visibility, but was then delayed when both navigators' tanks tumbled into bomb craters. (*Author*)

During the early hours of 8 August, Lt-Col Jolly's right forward column successfully advanced 3.9 km south-southeast across the fields of le Val, le Laumel, and la Sablonette, despite the problems posed by unseen craters and German fire, as well as by the dust-enriched darkness that caused the column to fragment. Around 0600 hours, Jolly halted his forces 500 metres short of their objective – Cramesnil – so that they could regroup and debus the infantry. The latter then advanced south-east across the open ground and then, as Jolly's tanks poured fire into the village, they stormed the German position. By 0730 hours the column had secured the village in the face of light opposition.

View taken from near the British right forward column's debus point north-east of Cramesnil looking into the village. Once at this location, Jolly's infantry debussed and then successfully stormed the village. *(Author)*

Deployed behind this force, the right rear column – 7th Black Watch and 148th RAC – only crossed the start line at 0015 hours, after Jolly's column had moved forward. With just 129 vehicles, the right rear column was smaller than its sister formation; as it was initially to follow the route cleared by Jolly's force through the German minefields, it lacked any flail tanks. During the first 105 minutes of its advance – during which it met only light resistance – the column followed Jolly's force for 2.5 km to reach the level crossing at Point 84. It then swung left across the railway and advanced 1.1 km east-southeast until it was within 500 metres of its objective, Garcelles-Secqueville. Here, at 0430 hours, the column's infantry – having debussed from their carriers – assaulted the village, and within an hour had secured it. Even though the column had established adequate defensive positions by 0700 hours, the ensuing 120-minute German artillery barrage on Garcelles-Secqueville nevertheless inflicted significant casualties. Overall, though, the British column assault on the offensive's eastern sector had achieved even greater success than that accomplished by the Canadian columns in the west. The three British columns had not only secured all their objectives, but had also done so with tolerable casualties – the left column, for example, suffered by far the most heavily with 11 killed and 58 wounded or missing. By mid-morning on 8 August, therefore, these British columns had dug themselves in along positions that constituted a 2,400-metre wide and 6,300-metre deep rupture of the German line.

Silhouetted by incoming sunlight, South Saskatchewan Private G.O. Parenteau takes up position in a haystack near Rocquancourt on 11 August. German snipers similarly concealed in haystacks around Garcelles-Secqueville inflicted casualties on 7th Black Watch on the morning of 8 August until 148th RAC Shermans knocked over the stacks to expose these hidden soldiers. *(NAC PA-128089)*

Like its Canadian neighbour, the 51st Division's break-in operation also involved foot infantry attacks, mounted by Brigadier Cassels' 152nd Brigade, to secure the localities by-passed by its columns. Meanwhile, 153rd Brigade remained deployed around Bourguébus, ready to consolidate the eastern flank by securing la Hogue if the Germans withdrew from this locality. Two of Cassels' three infantry battalions took part in these foot attacks. Lt-Col G.L.W. 'Geordie' Andrews' 2nd Seaforth Highlanders were to operate in the narrow axis located between the routes of advance of the right and left British columns. As described in Tour B, Stands B4–B5 (*see pp. 145–52*), the battalion was to advance 2,100 metres south-southeast from near Hubert-Folie to capture Tilly-la-Campagne. Meanwhile, 5th Cameron Highlanders would advance 3,600 metres south-southeast from la Guinguette to capture Lorguichon, and thus secure communication with the Canadian forces located to the west.

An ammunition truck burns fiercely near Cintheaux on 8 August. The fires that poured from several wrecked tanks of Lt-Col Jolly's column which had hit mines, plus the anti-aircraft tracer fired above the axis of Jolly's advance, meant that as 5th Cameron Highlanders advanced toward Lorguichon during the night of 7/8 August, the men found lack of visibility to be a less severe problem than those of many other units. (NAC PA-131374)

Marching south-southeast across the fields of la Chasse behind the two right columns on an axis 350 metres east of the main Caen–Falaise road, 5th Cameron Highlanders encountered only desultory German fire. Despite this, the battalion nevertheless only managed to advance 1,100 metres by 0100 hours thanks to the congestion created by the delays that Jolly's column had experienced. To surmount this problem, at 0130 hours Brigadier Cassels ordered the Camerons to move their axis of advance closer to the main road. Despite this change, the battalion nevertheless still only managed to progress slowly across the fields of le Laumel; the 90-cm high wheat that remained in these fields provided excellent cover for enemy snipers. The Camerons had to locate and deal with each sniper in turn before they could progress, and the battalion took as many as 35 prisoners in the process. It was thus not until 0330 hours that the battalion reached the northern fringes of Lorguichon. Two companies then launched a double-pronged frontal assault on the hamlet, while a third flanked east to secure the nearby woods. By 0445 hours, 5th Cameron Highlanders had secured Lorguichon without serious losses, and by 0900 hours the battalion had consolidated firm defensive positions ready to repel any counter-attack.

View from the outskirts of Cramesnil looking north-west across the fields of la Sablonette toward the south-east edge of the Lorguichon Woods. At 0340 hours on 8 August, two 5th Camerons companies assaulted the nearby hamlet of Lorguichon, while a third company struck south-east (toward the camera) to secure the woods. Although they rapidly secured the hamlet, they only managed to clear the woods at 0600 hours after meeting fierce resistance. *(Author)*

The corpses of six Canadian soldiers lie on stony ground awaiting burial on 9 August. The fact that II Corps incurred no more than 380 battle casualties during the successful break-in battle on 7–8 August vindicated Simonds' decision to employ novel and risky night-time infiltration tactics. *(NAC PA-132907)*

By noon on 8 August, therefore, the Allied attacks mounted on both the western (Canadian) and eastern (British) sectors during this first phase of Operation Totalize had undoubtedly secured resounding success. Five of the seven spearhead mobile columns deployed had secured their objectives, while the remaining two had dug in not too far away from these locations. In addition, two of the five marching infantry attacks had secured their objectives, while the remaining three would subsequently complete their missions later that afternoon. These latter delays demonstrated that at least some elements of 89th Infantry Division had fought with much greater determination that the Allies had expected. For the tolerable cost of 380 battle casualties, Simonds' novel night break-in offensive had secured a 7.4-km wide penetration of the initial German defensive position to an impressive maximum depth of 6.3 km.

With the benefit of hindsight, it seems that if Simonds' forces had abandoned their plans and instead mounted an improvised continuation of the break-in offensive that morning, they may have achieved considerable success. For their night attack had already shattered the initial German defensive zone, and the second defence line remained largely unmanned. Simonds' plan, however, understandably assumed that a successful assault on the supposedly potent second line was only feasible after a second bombing strike had occurred. Unfortunately, as this second bomb run was not due to begin until the early afternoon, there was an undesirable operational pause, during which the Germans could recover from the shock action inflicted by the Allied offensive.

Simonds, however, could not have brought these complex air support arrangements forward in time at such short notice. Alternatively, it would have still been an extremely controversial decision if Crerar – on Simonds' recommendation – had cancelled these strikes at this late stage. While it would have been difficult in practical terms – but not impossible – to recall hundreds of aircraft already in flight, politically it would have been all but impossible to cancel the air support for which Crerar had lobbied the reluctant bomber barons so long and so hard to secure. Most importantly, Simonds' available intelligence shed little light on the state of the second German line. Unlike subsequent historians, Simonds at this moment simply did not know how weakly held were the positions that faced his forces. The corps commander, therefore, lacked any compelling reason to do anything other than follow the original plan.

Some historians have viewed this as Simonds in effect eschewing the grasping of a fleeting opportunity to exploit the initial success gained by Totalize, in favour of a more cautious, firepower-reliant approach that seemed to fulfil the high command's desire to minimise casualties. Yet, if Simonds, the renowned 'thruster', here erred on the side of caution, it is hard to see any British or Canadian general within 21st Army Group who would have called this crucial shot any differently. Consequently, during the morning of 8 August, Simonds' spearhead forces sensibly consolidated their recent gains, while his two armoured divisions assembled behind them, ready to spearhead the offensive's second phase once the bombers had unleashed their cargoes of destruction. In the circumstances, this loss of Allied offensive momentum was essentially unavoidable.

CHAPTER 3

THE SECOND PHASE OF 'TOTALIZE'

During that fateful morning 681 USAAF B-17 Flying Fortresses steadily approached the Normandy coast. Their mission was to support the second phase of Totalize – the daytime break-in operation directed against the Bretteville–St-Sylvain defence line. As the lead pathfinder aircraft reached the Falaise plain, they identified the six aim points for the following bombers by dropping flares onto these targets while simultaneously Allied artillery fired red smoke rounds onto them. Subsequently, between 1226 and 1355 hours, 497 B-17s successfully delivered 1,487 tonnes of high explosive onto their targets. The remaining 184 bombers, however, had to abort their runs, some of them having been driven off course by the intense anti-aircraft fire put up by the III Anti-Aircraft Corps. The remaining aircraft – having failed to identify their targets with certainty due to the combination of thick dust, rising smoke, and patchy ground mist – aborted their missions rather than risk friendly-fire casualties. Indeed, to prevent the risk of 'blue-on-blue' casualties, the Allies had established a generous safety line, north of which the bombers were not to deliver their payloads. The line ran east for 3,100 metres from the quarry located 1,100 metres west-southwest of Gaumesnil through to Robert Mesnil, roughly 1,300 metres south of the current front line.

Despite these provisions, some tragic friendly-fire incidents still occurred. Unfortunately, flak hit the lead aircraft of the 351st Bomber Group and accidentally activated the aircraft's bomb release mechanism. In 1944, doctrine stated that, once the lead bomber had dropped its bombs, the other planes in that formation were to follow suit. Not realising that the lead plane had unintentionally delivered its payload, the rest of the formation released their bombs, which sadly fell on Allied lines. In this tragic accident, at least 65 Canadian and Polish troops were killed, and a further 250 wounded. In addition to causing widespread confusion and panic within the units affected, the incident undermined the morale of their soldiers. The Polish Division was particularly heavily hit by these incidents, and the subsequent lack of dash evident that afternoon among some of its sub-units may in part be explicable by the damage inflicted by this tragic accident.

As the Allies had anticipated, the USAAF's daylight strategic bombing attack during the early afternoon of 8 August encountered significantly heavier flak than that experienced the previous night. *(Imperial War Museum [IWM] HU91122)*

During the late morning of 8 August, while Simonds' forces regrouped as the Allied aerial armada approached the Falaise plain, local German commanders desperately attempted to organise a defensive response. Consequently, at 1130 hours, *Hitlerjugend* commander Kurt Meyer – then located north of Bretteville-le-Rabet – ordered *SS-Sturmbannführer* (Major) Hans Waldmüller to meet him at Cintheaux.

A few minutes later, while driving to this meeting, Meyer allegedly encountered dozens of infantrymen from 89th Infantry Division streaming south in disarray. In a now legendary scene, Meyer apparently stood alone but resolute on the main Caen–Falaise road, brandishing a carbine, and through his inspirational leadership rallied these stragglers to form new defensive positions around the village. This accomplished, Meyer then met up with General Eberbach, the Fifth Panzer Army commander, who had come forward to assess the battlefield situation. According to

Meyer, Eberbach then gave him full freedom of action to repel the Allied offensive. After this briefing had ended, Meyer met up with Waldmüller, and the two officers drove 1,200 metres north to the gentle rise situated north-east of Gaumesnil to determine the situation at the front. This was the perfect spot to observe the battlefield, and this attests to the advantages that accrued to the Germans due to their intimate knowledge of the local terrain.

By then, Meyer was already aware that Simonds' novel night assault had shattered the first German defensive line. Now the SS commander feared that the Allies would swiftly pass through massed armoured forces and drive south to smash through the as yet largely unmanned German reserve line that ran from Bretteville to St-Sylvain. I SS Corps had intended that, if the Allied attacks became too strong to hold, its front-line forces would withdraw in good order back to the second position, while *Hitlerjugend* units also moved into this line from the south. Simonds' night attack, however, had caught the Germans by surprise, and the rapid advance of his mobile columns had torn the heart out of the initial German position before significant forces had managed to withdraw. Now, as Meyer knew too well, this still weak second German line remained vulnerable to an audacious Allied armoured assault. As Meyer and Waldmüller surveyed the battlefield their worst fears were confirmed – in front of their eyes were deployed the armour from the mobile columns, plus behind them the spearhead elements of the two Allied armoured divisions, seemingly ready to strike south. Although both officers were battle-hardened SS fanatics, this awesome display of Allied military power so shocked them that, according to Meyer, it took their breath away.

For a few minutes, as he viewed the assembled Allied forces, Meyer could not fathom why this Allied armour had not commenced its attack south. Whatever the reason, Meyer concluded that his forces had to prevent this Allied armour from attacking south to break through the second German line, some 3 km south of the current front. If this position quickly collapsed, the Allied armour might be able to charge south to Falaise, and thus shatter the crucial hinge that supported the precarious German salient that jutted west toward Domfront. Thus, at around noon, Meyer – in typical SS leadership style – decided to fling all the *Hitlerjugend* units located in the vicinity into an immediate counter-attack. Despite being massively outnumbered,

The sight that horrified Meyer and Waldmüller. As they surveyed the battlefield from their vantage point near Gaumesnil around noon on 8 August, they saw neatly arrayed Canadian armoured columns, such as these, formed-up just 1.5 km away to the north-west, apparently ready to strike the fragile second German defensive line. *(NAC PA-113649)*

his forces might catch the Allies by surprise with the audacity of their riposte and hope to seize the initiative before the Allied leviathan commenced its attack. Through their daring and sacrifice, Meyer's teenage fanatics might buy precious time for other German reserves to move up and man the second defensive line.

Consequently, at noon Meyer ordered Waldmüller's battlegroup – reinforced by four Tigers from *SS-Hauptsturmführer* (Captain) Michael Wittmann's 2nd Company, 101st Heavy SS Panzer Battalion – to strike north at 1230 hours toward St-Aignan on an axis situated 150 metres east of the main road. Although these SS units had been largely untouched by the successful break-in phase of Totalize they were still outnumbered by the Allied armour now assembled opposite them. For, in the la Jalousie–St-Aignan sector across which this battle would rage, the Allies had deployed four armoured regiments and four infantry

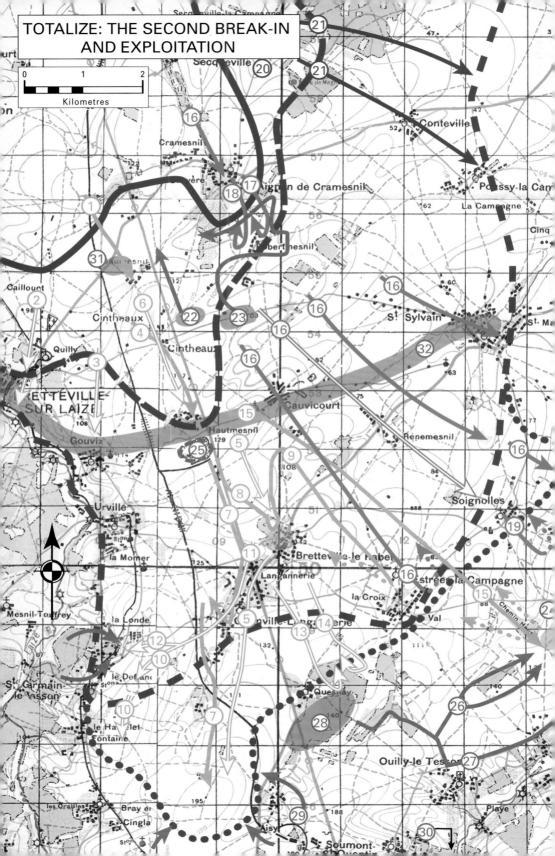

TOTALIZE: THE SECOND BREAK-IN
AND EXPLOITATION

0   1   2
Kilometres

①	4th Canadian Armoured Division	⑳	51st (Highland) Infantry Division sector
②	Calgary Highlanders	㉑	153rd Infantry Brigade
③	Régiment de Maisonneuve	㉒	Battlegroup *Wittmann*
④	Two troops, South Albertas	㉓	Battlegroup *Waldmüller*
⑤	Argylls of Canada	㉔	Battlegroup 85th Infantry Division and 1st Company, 12th SS Anti-Tank Battalion
⑥	A and D Companies, Argylls of Canada	㉕	HQ Company, I/25th SS Panzergrenadiers and elements 89th Infantry Division
⑦	Governor General's Foot Guards	㉖	Company, I/25th SS Panzergrenadiers and company, 12th SS Panzers
⑧	Halpenny Force	㉗	Company, I/25th SS Panzergrenadiers and two platoons, 101st Heavy SS Panzer Battallion
⑨	Canadian Grenadier Guards	㉘	Battlegroup *Wünsche* (bulk 12th SS Panzers)
⑩	Elements Lincoln and Welland Regiment	㉙	Battlegroup *Krause* (III/26th SS Panzergrenadiers)
⑪	Lincoln and Welland Regiment	㉚	Headquarters, 12th SS Panzer Division
⑫	D Company, Lincoln and Welland Regiment	㉛	Elements 89th Infantry Division
⑬	Queen's Own Regiment of Canada	㉜	Second German defensive line
⑭	North Shore Regiment		German defensive positions
⑮	Worthington Force		Allied front line, 1000 hrs, 8 August
⑯	1st Polish Armoured Division		Allied front line, 2359 hrs, 8 August
⑰	24th Polish Lancers		Allied front line, 2359 hrs, 9 August
⑱	2nd Polish Armoured Regiment		Allied front line, 2359 hrs, 10 August
⑲	9th Polish Infantry Battalion and 10th Polish Motor Battalion		Armoured forces / Infantry forces

Base maps: GSGS 4250 St Pierre sur Dives 7F4 , Falaise 7F6

battalions. At that moment, the elements of Waldmüller's task force deployed in this sector included Wittmann's 4 Tigers, 10 tank destroyers, 20 panzers attached from Battlegroup *Wünsche*, and around 500 panzergrenadiers.

By this date, Wittmann had become Germany's leading tank ace, but now the legendary commander was about to face his greatest test; unfortunately for him, the only force he had immediately available for this counter-strike was his own troop of four Tigers. At that moment, these Tigers were hidden under camouflage behind a tree-hedge in the les Jardinets area 600 metres east of Meyer's vantage point at Gaumesnil. On this day, moreover, Wittmann was in an unfamiliar tank – battalion commander *SS-Obersturmbannführer* (Lt-Col) Heinz von Westernhagen's command Tiger number 007 – as his own vehicle was being repaired. By choice, Wittmann normally eschewed use of a command Tiger because these vehicles carried 30 fewer rounds than the normal combat version due to the extra communication devices that they mounted. Wittmann, it would seem, preferred the enhanced fighting capabilities of the standard Tiger to the improved command and control facilities of the command variant. This preference, perhaps, may have reflected

A Canadian Ram artillery observation tank advances toward Cintheaux on the afternoon of 8 August. The forward observation officer deployed in such a tank would use the enhanced communications devices the tank carried – note the twin antennae – to call down supporting artillery fire. *(NAC PA-131776)*

some deeper SS leadership ethos – one that seemingly embraced heroic inspirational leadership rather than coolly calculated command and control.

At around 1220 hours, Meyer and Waldmüller were back at Cintheaux finalising the arrangements for this counter-attack, when Wittmann arrived for an oral briefing – no staff-produced documentation accompanied this hastily improvised riposte. At that moment, Meyer apparently recalled seeing a solitary Allied aircraft fly over their location several times sending out coloured flares. Meyer deduced that this was an Allied pathfinder aircraft marking the aim points for an impending strategic bombing strike – an attack that was probably less than 10 minutes away! Now Meyer knew why the Allied armour had not commenced its assault south. If his forces remained in their present positions, they would soon be pulverised by hundreds of tonnes of high explosive. Immediately after such a bombing strike, Meyer calculated, the Allied armour would pour south, quickly overrun his still dazed forces, and swiftly shatter the second German defensive line.

In these circumstances, Meyer realised he had but one choice. He later recalled shaking Wittmann's hand and ordered both him and Waldmüller to counter-attack north immediately with all available resources. From the experience he had recently gained fighting the Allies, Meyer knew that they left a generous safety zone between their own ground forces and the aiming points for their bombers. If Meyer's forces attacked the current Allied front they would enter this safety zone, and thus escape the bombing inferno that would fall harmlessly to their south. As Wittmann turned to leave, Meyer allegedly reminded the tank ace that, despite the unfavourable odds, success in this mission was essential if the German front, already ruptured by the first day of Totalize, was to stand any chance of being restored. Over the next 50 minutes, Wittmann strove to achieve this impossible mission by leading his Tiger troop in its desperate riposte. These dramatic events – including the warrior's death that befell Wittmann, possibly at the hands of Trooper Joe Ekins, gunner in a Sherman Firefly – are recounted in Stand C1 (*pp. 153–8*).

Tiger tank ace Michael Wittmann received the coveted Knight's Cross with Swords and Oak Leaves for his 139 'kills', made mainly on the Eastern Front. The Germans built up the Wittmann legend by publicising the bloody repulse his Tigers inflicted on the British 7th Armoured Division at Villers-Bocage on 13 June 1944. *(BA-299/1802/8)*

Meanwhile, elements of Battlegroup *Waldmüller* had assembled in the les Jardinets–les Ruelles area to execute their part in Meyer's daring counter-strike. This force, which comprised 20 tanks and 200 panzergrenadiers, aimed to strike due north to capture the high ground south of St-Aignan. The panzers therefore charged north across the open fields, only stopping occasionally in the few shallow gullies they encountered to engage the Allied vehicles concealed in the orchards south of St-Aignan. Behind them, the panzergrenadiers rushed forward to support the tanks, but then Allied artillery fire began to rain down on the area, forcing many of them to go to ground. The remaining infantry, however, continued to follow the lead panzers north until, by 1255 hours, the force had reached the various tree-hedges located north and north-northwest of Daumesnil. Using these as cover, the Germans continued to push north-northwest toward St-Aignan and the nearby orchards.

It was now that the Shermans of No. 3 Troop, A Squadron, 1st Northamptonshire Yeomanry – including Ekins' Firefly – spotted a group of Waldmüller's armour positioned 1 km due south, largely concealed behind some tree-hedges. Despite having only a slight target at which to aim, Ekins' Firefly nevertheless obtained a first-round hit on the lead panzer, causing it to brew up. Fearing the potent 17-pounder gun mounted on the Firefly, some of the remaining German tanks withdrew south. The remaining panzers, however, worked their way stealthily north-northeast using the cover provided by the nearby tree-hedges, and then infiltrated 900 metres south-west through le Petit Ravin – an unobtrusive defile situated 800 metres south of St-Aignan – to engage 1st Northants Yeomanry from the flank in a series of confused engagements. Allied mapping of the area was so poor that this defile was actually depicted as flat ground! Although Waldmüller's forces achieved some success, destroying around 20 Shermans, by 1340 hours intense Allied tank, anti-tank, artillery, and small-arms fire had eventually forced them to retreat south in some disarray after losing 11 panzers, including five precious Tigers. By 1400 hours, therefore, Waldmüller's forces had begun to dig themselves in back at their original starting positions – just as the massed Allied armour began to roll south.

Even though Meyer's bold scheme to disrupt the advance had failed, it seemed to him that it had stalled the Allied onslaught for a precious 90 minutes during which German forces could frantically dig in along the Bretteville–St-Sylvain line. In reality, however, the Allies had incorporated a generous margin to allow for the completion of the bombing – consequently, the armoured attack south was only due to start at 1355 hours. Thus, Meyer's counter-strike gained the Germans no additional time at all. It would be quite wrong, however, to dismiss Meyer's counter-strike as a pointless and costly exercise. Rather, this display of German daring in the face of overwhelming odds exerted a detrimental impact on Allied offensive determination that far outweighed any physical damage the attack had inflicted. This was the true achievement of Meyer's riposte, and it was this that helped make the afternoon of 8 August a fleeting battlefield opportunity that the Allies woefully failed to exploit.

For at 1355 hours, the spearhead units of 4th Canadian and 1st Polish Armoured Divisions respectively struck south along axes located west and east of the main Caen–Falaise road. Meanwhile, the remainder of these formations were struggling forward through congested traffic toward their forming-up-points. As the Canadian division advanced, however, some of its units experienced communication problems, which on occasion prevented them from calling down the pre-arranged artillery strikes designed to help them overcome the resistance they might encounter. In addition, the fire support available to these spearhead units was also limited because several artillery units had been disorientated by the recent friendly-fire bombing incidents. One battlegroup that experienced such difficulties was Halpenny Force, which comprised the Canadian Grenadier Guards – commanded by Lt-Col W.H. Halpenny – and a motor battalion, the Lake Superior Regiment.

Order of Battle: 4th Canadian Armoured Division
8 August 1944

Commander	*Maj-Gen George Kitching*
4th Canadian Armoured Brigade	*Brig E.L. Booth*

   21st Armoured Regiment (The Governor General's Foot Guards)
   22nd Armoured Regiment (The Grenadier Guards of Canada)
   28th Armoured Regiment (The British Columbia Regiment)

10th Canadian Infantry Brigade	*Brig J.C. Jefferson*

   The Algonquin Regiment
   The Argyll & Sutherland Highlanders of Canada
   The Lincoln & Welland Regiment
   The Lake Superior Regiment

Divisional units:
   29th Armoured Reconnaissance Regiment (The South Alberta Regiment)
   5th Anti-Tank Regiment, RCA
   15th & 23rd Field Regiments, RCA

Many of the unit commanders within these two divisions, moreover, had heard from their peers about the costly previous battles fought in Normandy, and held a healthy respect for German anti-tank capabilities. In addition, the problems experienced that afternoon with communications and fire

HISTORY

Above: Neat columns of armoured vehicles of 1st Polish Armoured Division lined up ready to strike south in the second phase of Totalize. *(IWM B8835)*

Inset right: 1st Polish Armoured Division commander, Maj-Gen S. Maczek, briefs press correspondents about the forthcoming Totalize offensive at Crerar's Amblie HQ on 7 August. During the operation's planning, both Maczek and Maj-Gen Kitching of 4th Canadian Armoured Division complained that Simonds had allocated their respective armoured divisions too narrow a frontage in Phase II of the offensive. *(NAC PA-1208046)*

support, not to mention the daring drive north recently begun by Waldmüller's forces, only served to reinforce the marked respect with which these officers regarded their enemy. All this understandably led 4th Armoured Division's unit commanders to advance cautiously that afternoon. When the advancing spearheads encountered various copses or hedges that might conceal lethal German anti-tank or tank assets, for example, they paused until their unreliable communications had managed to call down artillery to suppress these potential positions.

The combination of this offensive caution and the congestion caused as the armour passed through the infantry's front-line positions, so slowed the Allied advance that higher commanders soon demanded that their spearhead units generate greater forward momentum. Despite such exhortations, the methodical engagements executed by 4th Armoured Division's inexperienced troops still failed to generate the momentum expected – whether appropriately or not – by higher command. By late afternoon, this situation had left Simonds fuming and the hard-pressed Meyer exultant that the adverse battlefield situation he faced had not yet deteriorated into a dire one. Finally, 4th Armoured Division commander Maj-Gen George Kitching then came forward to see what was going on, as Brigadier Leslie Booth – the 4th Armoured Brigade commander – was not answering his radio. When he reached Booth's tactical headquarters, it is alleged that Kitching found the exhausted brigadier asleep in his tank. It is claimed that after rousing Booth and giving him a dressing-down, Kitching apparently ordered the brigadier to ginger up the advance of his troops. Yet this sense of urgency coming down the chain of command to the front only exerted a modest impact on the battlefield realities then unfolding at the offensive's cutting edge. At 1900 hours, for example, Booth ordered Halpenny's Canadian Grenadier Guards – supported by a Lake Superior Regiment company – to capture Bretteville-le-Rabet before darkness arrived. By the time that the task force's elements had assembled, however, it was already dark. Rather than risk his force by attempting this hastily improvised assault in darkness, Halpenny postponed the mission until dawn and instead followed current doctrine by withdrawing his tanks back to Cintheaux, where they safely harboured for the night.

During the late afternoon, however, one Canadian battlegroup did generate sufficient momentum to push south and secure

Then: A Canadian half-track towing a trailer passes through the southern apex of Cintheaux's (triangular) market 'square' on the afternoon of 8 August. At 1220 hours that day, as the massed B-17 squadrons approached Caen, the SS panzer-grenadiers who had followed Meyer into Cintheaux hurriedly redeployed into the fields to the north, which lay in the Allied 'bombing safety zone'. *(NAC PA-113655)*

Now: The author's car parked in the same spot as the half-track. As the SS panzer-grenadiers frantically dug shell-scrapes in the fields north of Cintheaux, the skies above filled with hundreds of Allied bombers. After witnessing this terrifying sight, a grenadier allegedly shouted to his comrades, 'What an honour, Churchill is sending a bomber for each one of us!' *(Author)*

HISTORY

Cintheaux and the northern part of Haut Mesnil. This task force comprised two Sherman-equipped troops from C Company, 29th Armoured Reconnaissance Regiment (South Alberta Regiment), plus infantry from A and D Companies, Argyll and Sutherland Highlanders of Canada. By 1600 hours, the battlegroup had teed-up a set-piece attack on Cintheaux, which went in soon afterwards. The assault soon secured success in the face of light enemy opposition; Lt Gerry Adams recalled that it was a very tame affair, during which his own tank never fired a single round. Afterwards, troop leader Adams concluded that the inexperienced South Alberta soldiers had prepared for this attack with excessive caution and an amateurish lack of co-ordination.

Having secured Cintheaux, the battlegroup then advanced 1.3 km to Haut Mesnil and the nearby quarry. By 1900 hours the force had secured the northern part of the village but could not

4th Canadian Armoured Division Shermans advance south near Cintheaux during the afternoon of 8 August. (NAC PA-140821)

push further south toward the quarry due to the intense resistance orchestrated from the nearby command post of 1st Battalion, 25th SS Panzergrenadier Regiment, part of Battlegroup *Waldmüller*. When, a few hours previously, Waldmüller had gone forward to meet Meyer at Cintheaux, his adjutant, *SS-Untersturmführer* (2nd Lieutenant) Willy Klein, had established an emergency blocking position around the battalion command post. Klein hastily formed a scratch force from the battalion staff company and reinforced it by forcibly intercepting a number of disorganised stragglers from 89th Infantry Division who were by then streaming south. For almost two hours that evening, Klein's force repulsed every Canadian attempt to secure the southern half of Haut Mesnil. Finally, some South Alberta Shermans tried to outflank Klein's position, but were soon caught by devastating 88-mm anti-tank fire that left several of them burning furiously. For Meyer, who had become concerned that Allied armour might break through at Haut Mesnil, had moved his two 88-mm-equipped flak batteries to new positions astride the main Caen–Falaise road some 2.8 km north of Potigny. As twilight descended, therefore, the exhausted Argyll and Sutherland Highlanders abandoned their assault and instead began to consolidate the positions they held in northern Haut Mesnil, while the South Alberta Regiment Shermans withdrew north to Cintheaux to harbour safely during the night.

As these Canadian operations unfolded, away to the east the 1st Polish Armoured Division also cautiously began to probe its way forward from 1355 hours. Two tank units from 10th Brigade – 2nd Polish Armoured Regiment and 24th Lancers – struck south and south-east from St-Aignan across the open fields north-east of Delle de la Roque. Both regiments attacked in tightly formed groups each with two 18-vehicle companies forward. Unfortunately, the Poles did not know that, after Waldmüller's abortive counter-strike, his tanks and anti-tank guns had concealed themselves behind the many hedges found around les Jardinets and Daumesnil to create a killing zone, into which the Polish tanks now headed. From 1435 to 1450 hours, the 1st Northamptonshire Yeomanry personnel deployed in the orchards around St-Aignan watched in horror as no fewer than 40 Polish tanks exploded into flames after being struck by long-range fire. This appalling introduction to the realities of war in Normandy forced the Poles to withdraw in disarray back into the shelter of the orchards located around St-Aignan.

1st Polish Armd Div (Pierwsza Dywizja Pancerna) 8 August 1944

Commander	*Maj-Gen Stanisław Maczek*
10th Armoured Brigade	*Colonel Tadeusz Majewski*
(10 Brygada Kawalerii Pancernej)	
1st Armoured Regiment *(1 Pułk Pancerny)*	
2nd Armoured Regiment *(2 Pułk Pancerny)*	
24th (Lancer) Armoured Regiment *(24 Pułk Ułanów)*	
10th Dragoon (Motor) Battalion *(10 Pułk Dragonów)*	
3rd Polish Infantry Brigade	*Colonel Marian Wroński*
(3 Brygada Strzelców)	
1st (Highland) Battalion *(Batalion Strzelców Podlalański)*	
8th Infantry Battalion *(8 Batalion Strzelców)*	
9th Infantry Battalion *(9 Batalion Strzelców)*	
Divisional units:	
10th Mounted Rifle Regiment *(10 Pułk Strzelców Konnych)*	
1st Anti-Tank Regiment *(1 Pułk Przeciwpancerny)*	
1st & 2nd Field Artillery Regiments *(1, 2 Pułk Artylerii)*	

After two hours of desperate reorganisation, the Poles courageously resumed their thrust south across the les Jardinets area. As the Polish armoured columns rumbled forward they passed the still-burning wrecks of their tanks destroyed in the earlier battle, which poignantly reminded them of the Germans' potent defensive capabilities. Undoubtedly, the combination of this painful battlefield experience and the damage done to troop morale, staff procedures and fire support arrangements by the earlier friendly-fire bombing accidents, sheds much light on why the Polish Division executed its subsequent operations that day in a cautious manner. Consequently, by dusk the Poles had only managed to advance 1.8 km to a line north of the road from Cintheaux to St-Sylvain.

Vehicles of the 1st Polish Armoured Division deploy to the south of Tilly-la-Campagne on 8 August, ready to spearhead the second, exploitation, phase of Totalize. *(NAC PA-128045)* .

The exonerating circumstances that the Poles legitimately claimed to explain their limited success that day – ones that did not apply to the 4th Division – cut little ice, however, with an increasingly frustrated Simonds. Although by no means an experienced armoured commander himself, Simonds had expected his armour swiftly to smash the second German line and then race south to secure the hills north of Falaise by evening. Moreover, with the assistance provided by the strategic bombing strike, Simonds knew that the afternoon of 8 August ought to have brought substantial Allied success. To Simonds, therefore, the 1,800-metre advance that the Poles achieved that day was even more lamentable than the paltry 3.8 km gained by 4th

Division. The modest *Hitlerjugend* units deployed against Simonds' armour had held up numerically superior forces and prevented an Allied breakthrough. Simonds' bitter disappointment at the apparent lack of drive displayed by his armoured forces lingered well beyond the remaining two days of Totalize. Indeed, this simmering anger erupted on 13 August during Simonds' briefing on Operation Tractable, during which he lambasted his subordinates for the alleged lack of determination evident during Totalize.

The Germans constructed extensive tunnels in the sides of Haut Mesnil quarry, in which they planned to store V2 and A9/A10 (Amerika) rockets. It was also used to store other equipment and weapons – including *Nebelwerfer* launchers. After the Argyll and Sutherland Highlanders and South Alberta Regiment captured the quarry on 8 August the Allies also used it as a storage depot. *(NAC PA-183132)*

Back on 8 August, Simonds' growing frustration manifested itself at 2100 hours when he – with scant regard for current doctrine – ordered his two armoured divisions to continue their attacks relentlessly throughout the night. In response, Kitching ordered Booth's 4th Armoured Brigade to advance 7.4 km that night to secure Bretteville-le-Rabet and the crucial high ground of Hill 195 (the modern Point 194), north of Fontaine-le-Pin. Booth entrusted the former mission to Halpenny Force, and the latter task to a still-to-be-formed all-arms grouping named Worthington Force. During the early hours of 9 August, both Canadian battlegroups hastily teed-up their various sub-units ready to resume their advance – despite the darkness – as per Simonds' impatient orders.

During this same night, the Germans – as was their practice in Normandy – took advantage of the lull in Allied fighter-bomber operations to redeploy and resupply their forces. The German defence now relied on the *Hitlerjugend* battlegroups, together with the badly-weakened – yet, perhaps surprisingly, still cohesive – 89th Infantry Division. In respect of the *Hitlerjugend*, Meyer ordered one half of Battlegroup *Krause* – 3rd Battalion, 26th SS Panzergrenadier Regiment – to withdraw and establish new positions on Hill 195. Simultaneously, the rest of the task force – formed around 1st Battalion of this same regiment – withdrew and established a new defensive line that ran north-east from the ridge by the Mines de Soumont across the south-west corner of the Hill 140 feature to Point 134, located 800 metres north of Ouilly-le-Tesson. As this redeployment unfolded, the Germans also used the cover of darkness to bring forward desperately needed ammunition stocks and food rations.

Meanwhile, Battlegroup *Waldmüller* – 1st Battalion, 25th SS Panzergrenadier Regiment and 1st Company, 12th SS Anti-Tank Battalion – established a new line that ran east-northeast from Point 134 across the southern slopes of the Hill 140 feature to the hills north of Maizières. Simultaneously, Meyer's remaining tanks and the six operational Tigers of 101st Heavy SS Panzer Battalion concentrated in Quesnay Wood, safely hidden from Allied air power. This position lay north of this new defensive line, and was designed to dominate any attempted Allied advance down the main road. As these forces redeployed, the division's artillery regiment and mortar battalion withdrew to new positions south of the River Laison. The division's command post

South Alberta Troopers J.L. Gaudet and G.A. Scott examine a road sign by the Caen–Falaise road at Cintheaux on 8 August. During Totalize the South Albertas operated as a fourth armoured regiment in 4th Division, instead of pursuing their assigned role of armoured reconnaissance. *(NAC PA-132413)*

remained sensibly located at the excellent vantage point of the Tombeau de Marie Joly, with another well-chosen observation point positioned immediately across the Laison gorge at la Brèche au Diable.

CHAPTER 4

THE FATEFUL ODYSSEY OF WORTHINGTON FORCE

While the *Hitlerjugend* redeployed during the night of 8/9 August, Worthington Force began a fateful 18-hour odyssey that would become the most tragic yet also the most heroic action of the entire Totalize offensive. This battlegroup comprised the 28th

HISTORY

Canadian Armoured Regiment (British Columbia Regiment), two embussed infantry companies from the Algonquin Regiment, and other supporting arms. The British Columbia commander, Lt-Col

One of the two memorials at the Worthington Force Monument, 1.5 km south-east of Soignolles beside the D131 road. *(Author)*

Donald Worthington, led the task force, which was named after him. At 0005 hours on 9 August, 4th Canadian Brigade ordered the task force to commence its night-time mission – a daring 7,300-metre advance south-southwest to seize Hill 195, the vital high ground north of Fontaine-le-Pin, located 10 km north of Falaise. The battlegroup was to secure this objective by dawn, so that it could establish sound defensive positions before the predictable daytime German counter-attacks began.

At 0400 hours on 9 August, Worthington Force set off from its assembly area around Gaumesnil and headed down the main Caen–Falaise road. C Squadron, British Columbia Regiment, led the vehicular column followed by the Headquarters Squadron, B Squadron, and finally A Squadron, with the two embussed Algonquin Regiment infantry companies interspersed among the armour. When the battlegroup had reached the Haut Mesnil area, the Clausewitzian friction that pervades night operations emerged with a vengeance. Here, Worthington Force rumbled into elements of Halpenny Force, which had encountered fierce resistance in its attack on Bretteville-le-Rabet. In what would turn out to be a fateful decision, Worthington swung his force south-east along an ancient raised grass track, the Chemin Haussé du Duc Guillaume, to avoid Halpenny's engagement. Having moved several kilometres south-east along this track, Worthington then intended to head south-west to rejoin the main Caen–Falaise road south of Grainville-Langannerie and from there continue the advance to Hill 195 as planned.

During the next 90 minutes, Worthington Force experienced a confusing night advance punctuated by sporadic German fire that emanated from all directions. In the darkness, the task force became horribly lost and inadvertently continued south-east along the Chemin Haussé instead of turning south-west. Eventually, at about 0530 hours Worthington's disorientated soldiers sighted through the gloomy half-light a glimmer of hope – high ground directly in front of them, but some way distant. With a sense of relief, they uncritically assumed that this must be Hill 195. The battlegroup increased speed and unwittingly continued south-east along the Chemin Haussé toward the hill, hoping to capture it before dawn ended the shroud of darkness that had hitherto concealed their advance. Yet, by then, the seeds of the disaster that was to engulf Worthington Force had already been sown, for the high ground it now approached was neither Hill 195 nor indeed any other hill remotely close to this objective.

View taken from near Point 88 at la Croix Midi looking south-east along the Chemin Haussé towards the woods north-west of the Worthington Force position. It is perhaps understandable how the battlegroup became so disorientated during its night advance. The grand title and centuries-old existence of the Chemin Haussé belie its modest physical realities on the ground. Given the darkness, it would have been difficult for Worthington Force even to detect that the track still existed, let alone ascertain their precise position. *(Author)*

In reality, by 0530 hours, the task force had reached a spot 1 km east-northeast and south-southwest, respectively, of Estrées-la-Campagne and Soignolles, somewhere near the fields of le Poirier. Worthington Force was then headed toward the les Trente Acres area around Points 111 and 122, located on the north-east corner of the Hill 140 feature (the modern Point 138). This ridge extended north-east from the Ouilly-le-Tesson–Estrées-la-Campagne area (where it merged with the north–south axis of the Cintheaux ridge) for 4 km until Rouvres, with its southern fringes descending into the steep wooded valley of the River Laison. Unfortunately for Worthington Force, les Trente Acres was located 4.8 km west of the main Caen–Falaise road, whereas its real objective – Hill 195 – was located 1.9 km east of this road. The battlegroup was therefore unknowingly closing on a hill that was situated a staggering 6.6 km north-northeast of its true objective!

At 0600 hours, as Worthington Force closed on Point 122, it entered the woods that straddled the Chemin Haussé north of le Gouloin. Here, the battlegroup surprised a small force from Battlegroup *Waldmüller*, destroying several armoured vehicles and killing 'many of the enemy' in the process. Next, with evident relief, Worthington's spearhead units stormed onto the undefended les Trente Acres area. Subsequently, at 0655 hours, the battlegroup radioed back to 4th Brigade the (incorrect) information that it had secured its objective – Hill 195. This force – which then amounted to three tank squadrons, one complete infantry company plus elements of a second, and supporting arms – then began to prepare defensive positions in readiness for daylight, when it expected to meet determined counter-attacks.

The fact that Worthington Force and the Allied higher command both wrongly believed that the battlegroup was then positioned on Hill 195 helped seal the latter's fate as it dug in around les Trente Acres. Unfortunately, Meyer and other SS officers located at the la Brèche and Tombeau observation posts had already detected the battlegroup as it approached Point 122, and *Hitlerjugend* units were already preparing counter-strikes to destroy the Canadian task force. As described in Stands C2–C4 (*see pp.* 159–68), over the next 14 hours the 'lost' Worthington Force courageously repelled repeated SS onslaughts. Lacking much assistance from friendly forces – the Allies directed some of their relief efforts onto Hill 195 – the heroic defenders of Point

122 could do no more than delay their inevitable decimation at the hands of numerically superior forces. By late evening it was all over, after a final German assault overran the last remnants of Worthington Force that still remained on the position.

Kurt Meyer (*right*) confers with Max Wünsche (*left*) and the then *Hitlerjugend* divisional commander Fritz Witt (*centre*) on 9 June 1944, earlier in the Normandy fighting. Witt was killed by British naval gunfire on the 12th, and Meyer took command of the division. Despite Meyer's reputation for ruthlessness, on 9 August – in a bizarre episode of shared humanity amid the horrors of battle – Meyer spent 30 minutes with captured British Columbia Regiment Captain J.A. Renwick amiably ruminating about 'the madness of war'. *(BA-146/88/28/259)*

While Worthington Force fought for its survival during 9 August, Totalize nevertheless unfolded elsewhere. Throughout that morning, Halpenny Force – the Canadian Grenadier Guards and Lake Superior Regiment – battled to overcome fierce resistance in Bretteville-le-Rabet. Then at 1300 hours, the Grenadiers withdrew from Halpenny Force and readied themselves to mount a rescue mission to assist Worthington's beleaguered command. Subsequently, at 1400 hours, C Company, South Alberta Regiment, and the Argyll and Sutherland Highlanders of Canada helped the Lake Superior Regiment overrun the last pockets of enemy resistance in Bretteville-le-Rabet. Meanwhile, back at 1300 hours, Kitching had ordered the 21st Canadian Armoured Regiment (Governor General's Foot Guards) to rescue Worthington Force by advancing rapidly down the main Caen–Falaise road to Hill 195. Between 1430 and 1500 hours, the Governor General's Foot Guards – supported by A Company, Algonquin Regiment – advanced south, overcoming weak resistance to reach the defile that ran north-northeast from Langannerie to Bretteville-le-Rabet. Here, the Canadians encountered an infantry company position bolstered by a Tiger tank and several anti-tank guns. During the next hour, the battle-group unsuccessfully strove to advance south. Eventually, one Foot Guards squadron tried to by-pass this resistance by mounting a right-flanking advance across the fields north-west of Vieille Langannerie. Exposed in the open ground, the Shermans met murderous 75-mm tank and anti-tank fire from Quesnay wood which halted their advance. Unable to get forward, and with darkness approaching, the Foot Guards withdrew north and redeployed into a defensive laager for the night.

View from Point 85 on the D239 road looking south-west across the fields of les Treize Acres toward la Croix church. At 1615 hours on 9 August, Canadian Grenadier Guards Shermans crossed these open fields in a bid to relieve the beleaguered Worthington Force, but met murderous German tank and anti-tank fire delivered both from the south and south-east; within minutes 26 wrecked Shermans littered this area. *(Author)*

Even while this futile rescue bid toward Hill 195 unfolded, the Canadians also attempted other relief efforts that reflected their growing suspicion that Worthington Force was actually somewhere near Hill 140, not Hill 195. At 1300 hours, the Canadian Grenadier Guards battalion had withdrawn from

Halpenny's attacks on Bretteville-le-Rabet to ready itself for such a rescue mission. By mid-afternoon, the Grenadiers had commenced their drive south-east from Cauvicourt toward Hill 140 and by 1605 hours they had advanced 2.1 km to reach the Bretteville–Soignolles road. As the Shermans crossed the exposed fields located between Bretteville and Estrées at about 1615 hours, however, they were caught by vicious German tank and anti-tank fire that knocked out 26 Shermans within a matter of minutes; not surprisingly, the surviving tanks withdrew north back out of this killing zone. This German defensive success therefore ensured that Worthington's troops were left to face their terrible fate alone.

Abandoned German vehicles litter Haut Mesnil quarry on 10 August 1944. During the previous morning, the Argyll and Sutherland Highlanders, backed by the Shermans of C Company, South Alberta Regiment, had cleared the quarry, before subsequently joining the Lake Superior Regiment in assaulting the last pockets of resistance in Bretteville-le-Rabet. (NAC PA-169295)

While 4th Canadian Division mounted these two relief missions, it also executed other operations to secure the starting points required for any subsequent drive toward the high ground around Fontaine-le-Pin. At 1500 hours, C Company, South Alberta Regiment, and the Argyll and Sutherland Highlanders advanced from Bretteville to assault Langannerie. Simultaneously, the infantry of the Lincoln and Welland Regiment, together with

A Company, South Alberta Regiment, struck south-west to assault the German positions in Vieille-Langannerie, Grainville-Langannerie, and Grainville. After a series of bitter engagements that involved intense close-quarters combat, the Canadian forces secured all four villages. In these battles, the lethal support provided by Allied Typhoon fighter-bombers proved particularly effective in softening up several pockets of resistance, with the result that thereafter 30 German soldiers promptly surrendered.

After these engagements, the Lincoln and Wellands and Argyll and Sutherland Highlanders began to dig in ready for the forthcoming hours of darkness, but then at 1900 hours Simonds ordered both battalions to continue operations throughout the night. From 2030 hours, the Lincoln and Welland Regiment was to advance 2.1 km south-west from Grainville-Langannerie and seize Hill 180 (now Point 179, near la Fontaine). Three hours later, the Argylls were to advance to capture the even more vital ground of Hill 195 – which by now, the Allies knew, Worthington Force had not secured. As the Lincoln and Welland Regiment advanced south the confusion created by the darkness and heavy German machine-gun fire caused its vanguard – D Company – to become lost and eventually end up in St-Germain-le-Vasson, 1,100 metres north-west of its intended objective. Their arrival stimulated fierce German ripostes that surrounded the isolated company, but unlike Worthington Force the group managed to hold out until relief forces arrived the next morning. Despite this setback, the rest of the battalion nevertheless reached the northern slopes of Hill 180 by late evening. Here, they spent the night establishing – 'as well as could be done in the dark' – a firm defensive base in readiness for the counter-attacks that daylight would, in all probability, bring.

Meanwhile, in preparation for its impending night advance toward Hill 195, Lt-Col Dave Stewart's Argyll and Sutherland Highlanders mounted several recce patrols, which revealed that the Germans had only established strong positions along the hill's western edge. Consequently, Stewart evolved a daring plan in which the battalion would execute a surprise silent night march onto the north-east corner of the hill. Having reached its objective without being detected, the Argylls would 'dig like hell' to establish strong defensive positions before dawn brought the predictable counter-attack. Between 0001 and 0500 hours, therefore, Stewart led his infantry single file in this silent infiltration onto Hill 195, avoiding contact wherever possible. Once successfully on the objective, the Canadian infantry – with the assistance provided by 12 press-ganged German prisoners – feverishly dug defensive positions in the short time that remained before dawn broke. By daybreak, moreover, some towed Canadian anti-tank guns had also reached the objective and were being dug in to bolster the position's defensive capabilities. In one of the most impressive actions of the entire offensive, the Argyll and Sutherland Highlanders had secured their objective without suffering a single casualty.

To exploit this success, Kitching then ordered the Governor General's Foot Guards to pass through the Argylls and advance 2.3 km south-east to secure Hill 206 (the modern Point 207) before the anticipated daylight German counter-strikes reached full intensity. As dawn broke, however, and before Kitching's plan could unfold, intense German anti-tank and *Nebelwerfer* fire rained down on the Highlanders' positions on Hill 195. Then panzergrenadiers of 3rd Battalion, 26th SS Regiment, mounted a series of furious assaults on the hill, assisted by Goliath remote-controlled demolition vehicles. Throughout the day, the hard-pressed Canadian infantry, anti-tank gunners, and Governor General's Foot Guards' Shermans, aided by artillery and tactical air support, drove off every assault on the hill. Yet this determined German response also made it clear that Kitching's orders to press forward to Hill 206 could not be realised – an appreciation soon underscored when Allied aerial reconnaissance detected 20 *Luftwaffe* 88-mm flak guns deployed in the area.

While these Canadian operations unfolded during 9 August, to the east of the main Caen–Falaise road the Polish Division also recommenced its advance south. Around noon, the Poles began to assault the German positions located around St-Sylvain and north of Soignolles. The I SS Corps' escort company, the *Hitler-jugend* escort company, and 1st Company, 12th SS Anti-Tank Battalion – all elements of Battlegroup *Waldmüller* – held this sector of the front. As the Polish tanks crossed the grain fields north-east of Renémesnil, *SS-Unterscharführer* (Sergeant) Leo Freund of the divisional escort company observed that German anti-tank fire knocked out several Polish vehicles. The armour nevertheless continued to advance south-east, and by 1400 hours had overrun not only the foxholes that Freund's platoon manned, but also the nearby company headquarters established under camouflage within a hollow in the ground. In this latter action, the wounded *SS-Unterscharführer* Kurt Breitmoser, the forward observer of the company's infantry gun troop, displayed outstanding courage by using an abandoned anti-tank gun to destroy several Polish tanks. Such bravery notwithstanding, by late afternoon the Poles had captured St-Sylvain and had outflanked the German positions around Soignolles. The battered remnants of the two escort companies, however, continued to offer desperate resistance from within Soignolles itself.

During the continuing Canadian advance of 9 August, this make-shift stand manned by Lance-Corporal Tom Armstrong gave directions to disorientated soldiers, such as Lance-Corporal John Macdonald, seen here in the background. *(NAC PA-160831)*

Meanwhile, 1 km further west, other Polish units also advanced south-west toward Estrées-la-Campagne. Indeed, it was probably these Polish tanks that, at around noon, inadvertently engaged Worthington's units deployed around Point 122. After the latter had fired off yellow identification rounds, the Poles began to suspect that this friendly unit was the missing Worthington Force, a belief confirmed at 1500 hours when Worthington's last eight operational tanks escaped back to the Polish lines. Consequently, the Poles redoubled their efforts to push on and rescue the stricken Canadian battlegroup. Despite these attempts, mounted throughout the afternoon and into the early evening, intense German fire prevented the Polish armour from advancing south-east beyond la Croix and Estrées toward Point 122. With the relief efforts mounted by the Canadian Grenadier Guards and the Poles both stymied by this determined resistance, Worthington Force was thus left to fight alone for its very survival in the face of repeated SS counter-attacks. During the course of the day, however, various small groups from Worthington's command did manage to make it back to the Polish lines.

During the subsequent morning of 10 August, a disappointed Simonds issued new orders designed to restore momentum to his corps' flagging advance. At 1600 hours, 3rd Canadian Division was to mount an improvised thrust south-east from Langannerie through Quesnay wood, across the Laison near Ouilly-le-Tesson, to secure Hills 184, 160, and 175 (the latter two the modern Points 161 and 174, respectively). The 2nd Canadian Armoured Brigade and two complete army groups Royal Artillery were to support the division during this attack. Due to delays in forming up, however, the 8th Brigade attack on Quesnay wood did not begin until 2000 hours. Despite the darkness and the dearth of intelligence concerning the enemy, the Queen's Own Rifles of Canada and the North Shore Regiment nevertheless fought their way into the northern fringes of the wood. Intense all-arms SS counter-attacks, however, soon drove them back out again, although elements of the North Shore Regiment fought doggedly throughout the night to retain a foothold in the wood. At dawn the surviving soldiers withdrew after a night of sustained combat and repeated friendly artillery fire that most felt was their worst ordeal of the entire Normandy campaign.

Simonds' hastily organised attempt to kick-start the stalled momentum of Totalize had proven to be a dismal failure, and so around 2200 hours on 10 August the corps commander terminated his stalled offensive. It was now clear to Simonds that II Corps had to reorganise its forces before it launched a new set-piece offensive toward Falaise.

By its termination, Totalize had secured up to a 15-km deep advance across a maximum frontage of 13 km. The Allied front now ran along the eastern bank of the River Laize from Bretteville through to Gouvix, then south-southeast to Hill 195 and north-northeast back to Quesnay, thence east to Estrées and north-east to Soignolles. Yet – critically – the operation's principal objectives – the high ground north of Falaise – remained unachieved, lying up to a further 8.1 km south of this front line.

CHAPTER 5

THE BACKGROUND TO 'TRACTABLE'

On 11 August, the day after Totalize ended, Montgomery issued a new directive to the First Canadian and Second (British) Armies that ordered them to drive 'quickly' toward Falaise and link up with the American forces then advancing north-east toward Argentan. Reflecting the urgency inherent in Montgomery's intent, this Directive M518 actually ordered both armies to strive for the capture of Falaise; this method maximised the chances that one of these two formations would secure this key road hub in a timely fashion. The directive aimed to effect the 'short envelopment' of German forces in the Falaise–Argentan area (to create the so-called Falaise pocket) – a concept enthusiastically

View from Rouvres bridge of the Laison River, which Allied intelligence dismissed as an insignificant obstacle. In reality, on 14 August, the stream proved more difficult to cross than anyone on the Allied side had anticipated. *(Author)*

embraced by Supreme Allied Commander Dwight Eisenhower. Instead of this short envelopment, however, Montgomery's preferred strategy was to execute a deep double envelopment of the German forces that would catch them against the physical barrier of the River Seine. He remained concerned that, if Allied forces attempted the short envelopment, they might be overrun as desperate Germans units fought their way out of the encirclement, aided by a synchronised break back-in operation mounted by forces located outside the pocket.

On receipt of M518, Crerar's First Canadian Army commenced the overarching staff planning required so that Simonds' II Corps could mount another offensive to capture Falaise. Initially, the operation was intriguingly codenamed 'Tallulah', presumably after the actress Tallulah Bankhead. Bizarrely, after 13 August, when the offensive's codename was altered to the militarily more meaningful 'Tractable', 4th Canadian Division continued to use the name Tallulah. Subsequently, an Canadian report caustically recommended that in future it might be sensible if all the formations involved in an offensive agreed on a common name for it! II Corps began planning Tractable on 12 August and, given the urgency inherent in M518, Simonds slated the attack to begin at noon on the 14th. This hasty planning no doubt explains why Tractable remained a modified repeat of Totalize: both offensives employed strategic bombing to assist the initial break-in; both exploited the restriction of enemy observation (whether through night operations, as in Totalize, or by smoke during daylight as with Tractable); and both used mobile spearheads that exploited shock action to overrun the initial enemy defences.

At the command briefings held on 13 August, Simonds demanded that his armoured subordinates ensure that Tractable secured Falaise quickly by pushing their commands to the very limits of endurance. This exhortation, which paid scant regard to current doctrinal norms, reflected Simonds' dissatisfaction with the offensive momentum generated during Totalize as much as it did the urgency imparted by Directive M518. Moreover, Simonds warned that he would not accept the fact that he had ordered doctrinally incorrect employment of armour as a valid excuse for the latter's inability to secure success. Put simply, the 'thruster' Simonds had made it clear that the only thing that mattered to him was that Tractable delivered success, and did so quickly.

Around 1130 hours on 14 August, Fort Garry Horse Shermans assembled at the Tractable start line near the gully located close to la Croix. *(NAC PA-113658)*

The final Tractable plan, therefore, based on Simonds' oral briefings, envisaged a two-phase operation that again aimed to dominate Falaise by capturing the high ground north of the city. To avoid the strong German position established in Quesnay wood, Simonds selected an axis of advance located 3.5 km east of the main Caen–Falaise road. Down this axis the 3rd Canadian Infantry Division grouping (*see box, p. 84*), deployed to the west, and the 4th Canadian Armoured Division grouping, positioned to the east, would strike south-southeast across a narrow 3-km frontage that ran from Estrées to Soignolles. Simultaneously, on the left (eastern) flank, 51st (Highland) Division was to mount an ancillary flank-protection attack against le Bû-sur-Rouvres.

During the offensive's first phase, Simonds' two leading armoured brigades were to charge 3.8 km deep through the German defences to establish bridgeheads over the River Laison, which Allied intelligence had indicated was not a major obstacle to vehicles. Two embussed Canadian infantry brigades would follow on behind the armour and establish a firm base along the Laison between Montboint and Maizières. Next, marching infantry from two additional Canadian brigades would pass through the positions established astride the Laison. Finally, during the offensive's second phase, Simonds' armour, backed by the marching infantry, was to advance up to 9 km south to capture the dominating high ground of Hills 184, 168 and 159, some 6 km, 4 km and 2 km north of Falaise, respectively.

Order of Battle: 3rd Canadian Infantry Division 14 August 1944

Commander	*Maj-Gen R.F.L. Keller*
7th Canadian Infantry Brigade	*Brig H.W. Foster*
The Royal Winnipeg Rifles	
The Royal Regina Rifles	
1st Battalion, The Canadian Scottish	
8th Canadian Infantry Brigade	*Lt-Col J.G. Spragge (acting)*
The Queen's Own Rifles of Canada	
Le Régiment de la Chaudière	
The North Shore Regiment	
9th Canadian Infantry Brigade	*Brig J.M. Rockingham*
The Highland Light Infantry of Canada	
The Stormont, Dundas & Glengarry Highlanders	
The North Nova Scotia Highlanders	

Divisional units:
7th Reconnaissance Regt (The Duke of York's Royal Canadian Hussars)
The Cameron Highlanders of Ottawa
3rd Anti-Tank Regiment, RCA
12th, 13th & 14th Field Regiments, RCA

Plus under command:

2nd Canadian Armoured Brigade	*Col J.F. Bingham*
6th Canadian Armoured Regiment (1st Hussars)	
10th Canadian Armoured Regiment (The Fort Garry Horse)	
27th Canadian Armoured Regiment (The Sherbrooke Fusiliers)	

To assist the break-in battle, Simonds again relied heavily on aerial support. For 15 minutes prior to the start of Tractable, medium bombers from the 2nd Tactical Air Force were to engage German tank, artillery, and mortar positions located along the Laison Valley at Montboint, Rouvres, and Maizières. To guide these bombers onto their targets, Allied artillery was to fire red smoke shells onto these areas. Then, from 1400 hours, 769 British and Canadian strategic bombers would strike six targets located along the attack's western flank, namely Quesnay wood, the villages of Aisy, Bons-Tassilly, Fontaine-le-Pin, and Soumont-St-Quentin, as well as the woods south-west of Hill 206. The

impact of these strikes was somewhat reduced, however, because late on 13 August German troops obtained documents from the corpse of a Canadian officer that indicated the approximate form that Tractable would take. Although in the time available there was only so much the Germans could do to exploit this valuable intelligence, they did manage to redeploy some forces, including sending an additional anti-tank gun battery to the Laison Valley. This latter move may account for the significant losses that some Allied armoured units suffered during their charge to the Laison.

On the morning of 14 August, the two divisional groupings involved in Tractable moved forward under strict radio silence to their assembly areas located between the Cauvicourt–St-Sylvain road and the start line along the Estrées–Soignolles road. By 1130 hours, these two groupings had between them assembled in this area a force of 480 tanks, 1,500 vehicles, and 12,000 troops, now ready to strike south into the soon-to-be-generated Allied smoke screen. These assembly areas were located on the northern slope of the Hill 140 feature, and thus the Germans – deployed on the southern slopes of the ridge – could not observe this forming-up process. As in Totalize, to maintain unit cohesion while moving with impaired visibility, the assault forces formed up into dense vehicle columns. Unlike the intimate all-arms groups employed in Totalize, however, on 14 August the armoured regiments spearheaded the attack, followed by discrete embussed infantry columns.

The two divisional groupings each deployed three distinct brigade-sized echelons of forces. The western (3rd Canadian Division) grouping deployed in its three echelons the 2nd Canadian Armoured, 9th Canadian Infantry, and 7th Canadian Infantry Brigades (*see box, p. 86*). These forces formed up to a depth of 3 km along a 1,300-metre front that ran east-northeast from Estrées to la Robe Noire, located 900 metres south-west of Soignolles. At noon, 2nd Brigade was to advance with the Fort Garry Horse and 1st Hussars deployed to the right and left, respectively. Next, at 1215 hours, the Highland Light Infantry of Canada and the Stormont, Dundas, and Glengarry Highlanders were to spearhead the 9th Brigade advance. The North Nova Scotia Highlanders and the attached 7th Canadian Reconnaissance Regiment (Duke of York's Royal Canadian Hussars) were then to follow on, while 7th Brigade meanwhile held its position for several hours until requested to move forward. These nine units were to advance 3.8 km south-southeast to establish a bridgehead over the Laison between Montboint and Rouvres, and then drive a further 3.9 km south-southwest to secure the vital high ground of Hills 184 and 170 (the latter, the modern Point 168).

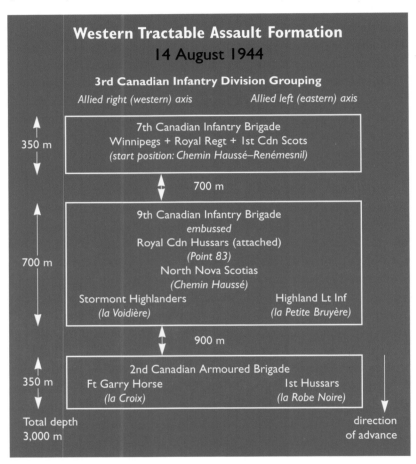

Western Tractable Assault Formation
14 August 1944

3rd Canadian Infantry Division Grouping

Allied right (western) axis   *Allied left (eastern) axis*

350 m

> **7th Canadian Infantry Brigade**
> Winnipegs + Royal Regt + 1st Cdn Scots
> *(start position: Chemin Haussé–Renémesnil)*

700 m

700 m

> **9th Canadian Infantry Brigade**
> *embussed*
> Royal Cdn Hussars (attached)
> *(Point 83)*
> North Nova Scotias
> *(Chemin Haussé)*
> Stormont Highlanders   Highland Lt Inf
> *(la Voidière)*   *(la Petite Bruyère)*

900 m

350 m

> **2nd Canadian Armoured Brigade**
> Ft Garry Horse   1st Hussars
> *(la Croix)*   *(la Robe Noire)*

Total depth
3,000 m

direction
of advance

Some 1 km further east, the 4th Canadian Armoured Division grouping also assembled during the morning in three echelons formed respectively by the 4th Canadian Armoured, 8th Canadian Infantry, and 10th Canadian Infantry Brigades (*see box opposite*). These forces deployed to a depth of 2.6 km across a 1-km front that ran east-northeast from near Soignolles to Point 85. The 4th Brigade was to advance with the Canadian Grenadier Guards and Governor General's Foot Guards on the left and the right, respectively, followed by the reconstituted British Columbia Regiment and the division's motor battalion, the Lake Superior

Regiment. Behind these units, 8th Brigade (from 3rd Canadian Infantry Division) was to advance with the embussed Queen's Own Rifles and le Régiment de la Chaudière on the left and right, respectively, followed on foot by the North Shore Regiment. Finally, 10th Brigade – backed by the South Alberta Regiment – would strike south. The division's intent was that these 11 units would advance 4.2 km south-southeast to establish a bridgehead over the Laison between Rouvres and Maizières, and then thrust up to a further 10 km south to capture Hills 175, 168 and 159, together with the villages of Épaney, Olendon, and Perrières.

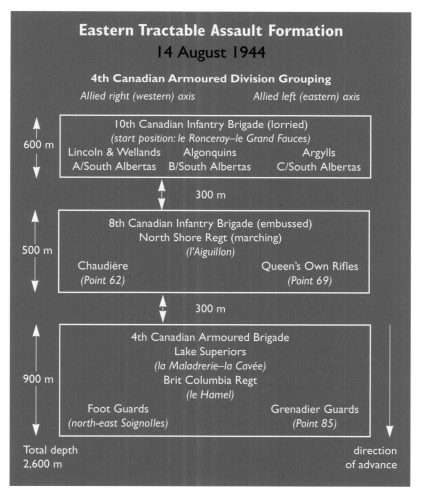

Eastern Tractable Assault Formation
14 August 1944

4th Canadian Armoured Division Grouping

Allied right (western) axis   *Allied left (eastern) axis*

↑
600 m
↓

10th Canadian Infantry Brigade (lorried)
(start position: le Ronceray–le Grand Fauces)
Lincoln & Wellands   Algonquins   Argylls
A/South Albertas   B/South Albertas   C/South Albertas

↕ 300 m

↑
500 m
↓

8th Canadian Infantry Brigade (embussed)
North Shore Regt (marching)
(l'Aiguillon)
Chaudière   Queen's Own Rifles
(Point 62)   *(Point 69)*

↕ 300 m

↑
900 m
↓

4th Canadian Armoured Brigade
Lake Superiors
(la Maladrerie–la Cavée)
Brit Columbia Regt
(le Hamel)
Foot Guards   Grenadier Guards
(north-east Soignolles)   *(Point 85)*

Total depth
2,600 m

direction
of advance

By 14 August the I SS Panzer Corps was in an even less advantageous position to repel this powerful Allied assault than it had been to halt Totalize. The remnants of the 89th Division, decimated during Totalize, for example, could now only man a paltry 2-km sector of the front west of the Caen–Falaise road. During 10–11 August, however, the corps had welcomed much-needed reinforcements, when the 85th Infantry Division took over the positions held by the *Hitlerjugend* east of the main road.

Order of Battle: Hitlerjugend Division 14 August 1944

Battlegroup *Krause* (SS-Sturmbannführer Bernhard Krause)
Elements 12th SS Panzer Regiment	*(approx 15 Panzer IVs and 9 Panthers)*
1st Coy, 12th SS Anti-Tank Bn	*(approx 7 Panzerjäger IV tank destroyers)*
2nd Company, 101st SS Heavy Panzer Bn	*(approx 4 Tigers, corps troops)*
1st Battalion, 25th SS Panzergrenadier Regiment	
Elements 1st and 3rd Bns, 26th SS Panzergrenadier Regiment	
12th SS Escort Company	
101st SS Escort Company	*(corps troops)*
Reconnaissance Group *Wienecke*	
12th SS Anti-Aircraft Battalion	*(4 x 88-mm, 9 x 37-mm AA guns)*
12th SS Mortar Battalion	
12th SS Artillery Regiment	*(four weak batteries)*
Total:	**2,500 personnel (including 400 infantry) 35 AFVs**

85th Infantry Division was a sister formation to the 89th, and Allied intelligence did not expect it to resist Simonds' new offensive effectively. The corps thus now had to rely on the *Hitlerjugend* as the mainstay of its defence, but by 14 August this force – now consolidated around Battlegroup *Krause* – only possessed the strength of a weak regimental group – about 2,500 men with just 400 panzergrenadiers and 35 operational AFVs.

Overall, the forces available to the I SS Corps to resist Tractable could only be categorised as modest.

The corps' defensive system comprised a 4.9-km deep zone with two separate positions. In the first line, elements of the 85th Division formed a fragile 600-metre deep infantry screen that ran east along the southern slopes of the Hill 140 ridge. Some 900 metres south of this line, the Germans had established a 3.4-km deep second defensive position. In this line, well-concealed *Hitlerjugend* units deployed throughout the wooded Laison Valley formed a potent anti-tank screen, which was augmented by a few *Luftwaffe* 88-mm flak guns. Finally, along the reverse slopes in the southern fringes of this screen, the Germans had concentrated the artillery of the 85th and *Hitlerjugend* Divisions, as well as their remaining *Nebelwerfers*. Beyond this zone, however, the Germans lacked any reserves in the mere 18 km gap that then remained between Falaise and the south-facing German front that opposed the American drive north toward Argentan. Whether these modest German defences would prove sufficient to prevent Simonds' forces reaching Falaise remained to be seen.

To help his assault forces get across the Laison River, Simonds deployed the British fascine-carrying AVRE vehicles of the 80th Assault Squadron, Royal Engineers, a part of the specialised 79th Armoured Division. These engineer tanks carried tightly-bound bundles of staves that could be released into a stream or anti-tank ditch to make a temporary crossing. *(NAC PA-116523)*

CHAPTER 6

OPERATION 'TRACTABLE'

Tractable began at 1137 hours on 14 August, when Allied artillery fired red smoke shells onto the German positions at Montboint, Rouvres, and Maizières to identify these targets for the 53 Allied medium bombers that struck these locations at 1145 hours. Then from 1155 hours, as these strikes ended, hundreds of Allied artillery guns delivered a mixed barrage of smoke and high explosive rounds across a 4,300-metre wide by 4,600-metre deep area that extended south from the line Point

①	Royal Winnipeg Rifles	⑬	South Alberta Regiment
②	1st Canadian Scottish	⑭	Régiment de la Chaudière
③	Regina Rifle Regiment	⑮	North Shore Regiment
④	Duke of York's Royal Canadian Hussars	⑯	Queen's Own Regiment of Canada
⑤	Stormont, Dundas and Glengarry Highlanders	⑰	Lake Superior Regiment
⑥	North Nova Scotia Highlanders	⑱	Governor General's Foot Guards
⑦	Highland Light Infantry of Canada	⑲	British Columbia Regiment
⑧	Fort Garry Horse	⑳	Canadian Grenadier Guards
⑨	1st Hussars	㉑	3rd Canadian Infantry Division sector
⑩	Lincoln and Welland Regiment	㉒	4th Canadian Armoured Division sect
⑪	Argylls of Canada	㉓	51st (Highland) Infantry Division
⑫	Algonquin Regiment		Base map: GSGS Operation Totalize

111–Bû-sur-Rouvres down to the line Montboint–Point 81. The gunners intended to create an 'impenetrable' density of smoke on the flanks of the barrage and 'mist' density elsewhere, but the advancing troops later reported variable results with the degree of visibility varying from 200 metres down to as little as just three metres. Meanwhile, back at 1142 hours, the terse order 'Move now' ended the Canadian forces' adherence to radio silence. In response, the first echelon of Simonds' two groupings – 400 tanks deployed in five regiments, plus a motor battalion – rumbled south at 18 km/hr towards the start line. Some 15 minutes later, the second echelon – one marching and five embussed infantry battalions, plus one recce regiment – moved forward. By 1200 hours, therefore, by which time the four leading armoured regiments had crossed the offensive's start line, 13 Canadian units were already moving south across the open fields in dense phalanx-like formations.

At 1205 hours, on the western axis, the Shermans of the Fort Garry Horse and 1st Hussars rumbled south into the smoke toward the Laison at Montboint. The tanks encountered only sporadic German resistance, thanks to the Allies' deliberately obscuring the battlefield and the suppressing effect of their aerial and artillery fire. On the other hand, thanks to the intelligence garnered the previous evening, the German tank and anti-tank gun crews deployed along the Laison knew the direction in which the Allies would advance, and had prepared their defensive fire

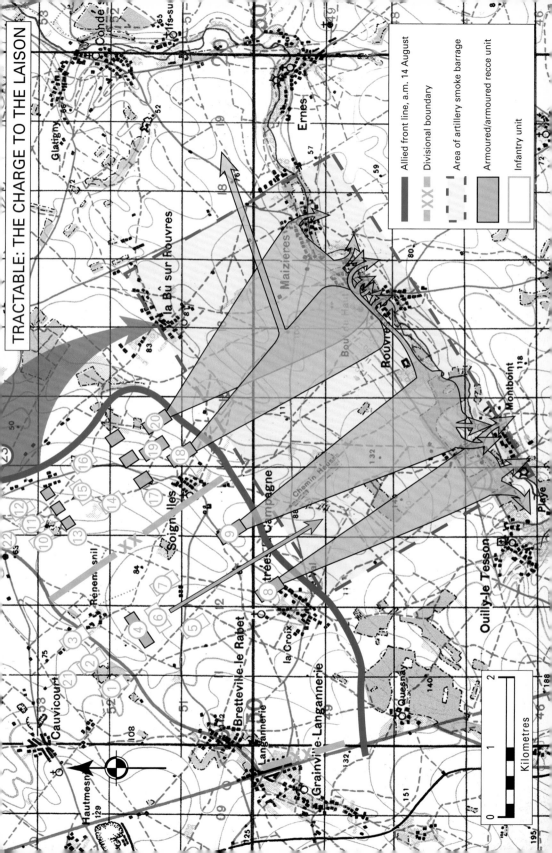

TRACTABLE: THE CHARGE TO THE LAISON

Allied front line, a.m. 14 August

Divisional boundary

Area of artillery smoke barrage

Armoured/armoured recce unit

Infantry unit

Kilometres
0   1   2

Vehicles of the western (3rd Division) grouping's second (embussed) echelon kick up dust as they move forward to the Tractable start line around noon on 14 August. In the foreground can be seen carriers towing 6-pounder anti-tank guns. *(NAC PA-116536)*

tasks accordingly. Despite often not being able to identify targets in the gloom, the German gunners nevertheless fired away at what they knew must be massed Allied formations, and by such methods accounted for 20 Shermans. Irrespective of these losses, however, the Canadian vehicles continued to head south through the smoke, overrunning many German trenches in the process. Dazed by the sight of hundreds of Allied vehicles streaming towards them through the smoke, many German infantrymen cowered in their trenches as the armour passed by them, and then promptly surrendered to the following Allied infantry forces.

During the first hour of Tractable, therefore, German resistance represented less of a threat to the forward momentum of the western grouping than did the difficulty of maintaining effective command and control on a smoke-filled battlefield. Just as in Totalize, the movement of hundreds of Allied vehicles across parched fields produced dense dust clouds. When these combined with the smoke barrage and the fumes generated by burning vehicles, visibility in places dwindled to almost nil. Allied drivers soon discovered that the only way they could navigate visually was to use the sun, which they could just make out through the intense gloom. Amid scenes of utter confusion, 2nd Brigade's columns disintegrated. The rear unit of 1st Hussars, for example, inadvertently overtook its spearhead A and C Squadrons, while the light recce vehicles of the Royal Canadian Hussars unwittingly overtook the vanguard of the Fort Garry Horse.

During the Canadian armoured charge toward the Laison mounted on 14 August, several Shermans became immobilised like this one, which previously had fallen into a deep bomb crater. Three Shermans of Lt Coles' 1st Hussars troop, for example, toppled down into a German anti-tank ditch that their crews failed to spot in the smoke-drenched battlefield. (NAC PA-113707)

Notwithstanding this chaos, many Canadian vehicles did manage to navigate themselves successfully toward their first objective, the Laison River. Indeed, by 1230 hours, the lead vehicles of the western grouping – those of the Royal Canadian Hussars – had reached the stream's northern bank, joined 15 minutes later by the entire 1st Hussars. Although the Laison in this sector was an innocuous, two metre-wide stream with a depth of just 20–70 cm, the 1st Hussars' crews became the first Allied personnel to discover that it was a more formidable obstacle than Allied intelligence had led them to believe. As the regiment's lead tanks attempted to ford the shallow stream they bogged down in its soft bed. Allied planning had recognised the need for bridging equipment, and so fascine-carrying tanks were to advance toward the stream in the wake of the second echelon.

From Rouvres bridge looking north-east along the course of the Laison toward the hamlet of le Bout de Haut. While Gordon's 1st Hussars squadron struggled across this damaged bridge, the regiment's depleted A Squadron crossed the stream using the bridge at le Bout de Haut and elements of its dispersed C Squadron forded the Laison at a spot an additional 300 metres east. *(Author)*

At 1255 hours, Major G.W. Gordon's B Squadron, 1st Hussars, decided not to wait around Assy until fascines had been put down across this obstacle. Instead, it advanced 1 km north-east along the northern bank to locate a safe crossing point or, if this failed, to cross the stream at Rouvres via the bridge there. Unfortunately, the former quest proved problematic because the woods along some parts of the northern bank made it difficult for tanks to drive down to the stream – this bank is now less densely wooded than it was in 1944. In other locations the stream's banks were high and steep which meant that, as tanks tipped into the stream, they risked bogging down. Elsewhere – as at Montboint – German fire covered the obvious crossing points. Finally, even if the tanks managed to surmount these difficulties, the crews did not know if the stream's soft bed would support the tanks' weight. The training the 1st Hussars had undertaken back in Britain, moreover, had stressed that crews should not risk bogging down their tanks by traversing unsuitable terrain.

Given this, it is understandable that Gordon eschewed risky attempts to ford the Laison and instead choose the apparently safer option of using the bridge at Rouvres. As described in Stand D2 (*see pp. 172–5*), however, when B Squadron reached Rouvres it discovered that the bridge was badly damaged. This forced Gordon to take a gamble no less serious than that of attempting to ford the stream; despite warnings from Allied engineers that the bridge was unsafe, at 1400 hours his Shermans carefully inched their way across the weakened structure. Just prior to this, the remaining mass of 1st Hussars – the badly depleted A and C Squadrons – had also reached Rouvres, having followed Gordon's squadron east-northeast along the northern bank in search of a crossing point. Believing the bridge to be damaged beyond use, however, these units continued along the northern bank until they managed to cross the Laison at two sites located 700 metres and 1,000 metres east of Rouvres. The tanks then reorganised themselves into a full-strength composite A/C Squadron in the open fields situated south of the river.

Back at 1315 hours, as the lead Shermans of the Fort Garry Horse also attempted to ford the Laison west of Montboint, they too bogged down on the stream's soft bed. Next, one Fort Garry Horse squadron approached the nearby road bridges that spanned the twin courses of the stream at Montboint, but found the area defended by determined infantry backed by machine guns. As the tanks then lacked infantry support, the squadron commander decided not to risk storming the bridge for fear of incurring losses from *Panzerfausts*. Instead, the force divided, some tanks heading south-west, the others north-east, along the northern bank in search of a spot to ford the stream. Eventually, the Fort Garry Horse discovered a minor bridge 900 metres further east, near le Logis Château, and by 1440 hours two of its squadrons had managed to get across. Armoured Vehicles Royal Engineers (AVREs) from 80th Assault Squadron, later reinforced this fragile structure by laying fascines across the stream. The two Fort Garry squadrons then reorganised themselves in a clearing south of the stream, ready to push on south toward Hill 184.

Meanwhile, between 1400 and 1530 hours, 417 Lancaster and 352 Halifax strategic bombers delivered 3,723 tonnes of high explosive onto six targets located west of the main Caen–Falaise road. Sadly, during these strikes friendly-fire incidents occurred that proved even more costly than those that had marred

Totalize. On this occasion, 77 bombers inadvertently dropped their bombs short onto the Allied positions, killing around 100 soldiers and wounding 300 others, including another substantial contingent from the unfortunate Polish Division. The fact that these losses had in part been caused by astonishing lapses in Allied inter-service communication only served to compound the tragedy. When the ground units found themselves being bombed, they had fired standard yellow friendly-forces identification flares, unaware that the Pathfinder aircraft were that day using yellow smoke to identify their targets to the following bombers! Apparently, Bomber Command had not been notified that it was army practice to use yellow smoke for identification purposes.

Prior to these events, the western grouping's second echelon – the embussed infantry of 9th Brigade, plus the Royal Canadian Hussars – had followed the preceding armour south across the start line at 1220 hours. The embussed Stormont, Dundas, and Glengarry Highlanders and Highland Light Infantry spearheaded this advance, deployed on the right and left axis, respectively. The Highlanders headed south-southeast across the summit of Hill 140 toward Assy, while the Highland Light Infantry advanced astride the Chemin Haussé, passing the Worthington Force vehicles wrecked on 9 August that still littered the area. In the poor visibility, however, the Highland Light Infantry became dispersed: B Company veered off into the path of the Highlanders, while C and D Companies blundered east for 4.8 km across the 4th Division axis until they neared Ernes. The Highlanders' advance proved less problematic, and by 1255 hours the infantry had debussed in the woods that bordered the Laison around Assy. During the afternoon, one of the battalion's companies successful advanced 2.1 km south-west along the stream's northern bank toward Ouilly-le-Tesson and St-Quentin, taking many demoralised prisoners in the process. Simultaneously, the battalion's B and C Companies overcame the German positions located around Assy and Assy Château. Next – as described in Stand D3 (pp. 175–9) – when B Company then tried to push west from Assy Château to seize the road bridge over the seasonal (northern) course of the Laison near Montboint, it found itself facing a seemingly intractable tactical problem. Around 1700 hours, however, the company cleverly resolved this dilemma by employing three fearsome Wasp flame-throwing vehicles.

Some of the 480 tanks deployed at the start of Tractable. This mixed group, probably from 2nd Canadian Armoured Brigade, fields an M10 tank destroyer and a Churchill Crocodile, as well as Sherman and Churchill tanks. *(NAC PA-116525)*

Meanwhile, as described in Stand D1 (*pp. 168–72*), between 1200 and 1220 hours the first echelon of the eastern (4th Division) grouping – 4th Armoured Brigade – advanced through the smoke to the west–east route of what is now the D131 road. During the next 35 minutes, however, the spearhead Governor General's Foot Guards and Canadian Grenadier Guards became intermixed and dispersed as they advanced south-east to reach the 2 km stretch of the Laison between Rouvres and Maizières. Some Shermans, indeed, became so spectacularly lost that they eventually crossed the Laison at Ernes and Ifs-sur-Laison, 3 km east of Maizières. Then, from 1305 hours, the 4th Brigade discovered that this babbling brook was a major tank obstacle, having met the same problems – wooded approaches, steep banks, German defensive fire, and soft stream bed – encountered by the western grouping. Nevertheless, over the next three hours, most of these 240 tanks eventually crossed the Laison using either the fascine-reinforced Rouvres bridge, one of the two fascine crossings established east of this village, or one of several safe fording places that had been located. Once across, the disorganised elements of 4th Brigade had to spend the next hour rearranging themselves into coherent tactical formations, and so it was not until around 1630 hours that these Shermans were ready to resume their advance south toward Hills 168 and 159.

Meanwhile, back at 1245 hours, the eastern group's second echelon – the one marching and two embussed infantry battalions of 8th Brigade – crossed the start line. The two mobile battalions passed the lateral road to Maizières at around 1305 hours, and subsequently reached the Laison 25 minutes later. The battalions' troop-carrying vehicles also experienced problems crossing the Laison, and therefore most of them debussed their troops on the stream's northern bank, forcing the infantry to continue the advance on foot. Finally, the grouping's third echelon – the three lorried battalions of 10th Infantry Brigade – only crossed the offensive's start line at 1510 hours, and thus only reached the Laison after a confused approach march by 1600 hours.

One tactical advantage of the Crocodile tank was that – in addition to its flame-throwing capabilities, as seen here – the vehicle could perform as a standard battle tank. This proved invaluable at Assy on the afternoon of 14 August, when the 75-mm rounds fired by two 141st RAC Crocodiles helped the Stormont, Dundas and Glengarry Highlanders fight off two Tiger tanks. *(TTM 2226/C2)*

The 2nd Armoured Brigade also only became ready to resume its advance south from the Laison around Assy toward Hill 184 at 1630 hours, after spending an hour on essential reorganisation. Around this time the Fort Garry Horse moved off from the clearing situated 900 metres east-northeast of Montboint, and subsequently advanced 2.6 km south-southwest across rising terrain to reach the eastern fringe of Hill 160 (the modern Point 161) by 1715 hours. The Fort Garry Horse, with the infantry of the Royal Winnipeg Rifles marching south some distance behind them, then pushed on to reach Points 178, 173, and 155 (close to the modern D242 road) just as darkness approached. Here, the Fort Garry Horse drew intense fire from the *Hitlerjugend* escort company, and so the tanks halted and established defensive positions for the night. In an impressive charge forward, the Fort Garry Horse had covered 4.3 km and now were only 600 metres short of the summit of Hill 184.

As Major Gordon's 1st Hussars squadron advanced south-southwest from its positions at Rouvres during the early afternoon, it encountered intense German fire delivered from the east that forced it to withdraw after taking losses. Next, seeing a Fort Garry Horse squadron pushing forward on its right, the squadron advanced once more toward Point 111, but fierce defensive fire again compelled it to withdraw. Eventually, the squadron – now down to just nine operational tanks – mounted a third drive up the hill that bore fruit, after the tanks overran an anti-tank gun position. Meanwhile, the regiment's composite A/C Squadron had also pushed south-southwest toward Point 111 from the area south of le Bout de Haut. During that evening, both squadrons then thrust south-southwest toward their objective, the north-east fringe of the Hill 184 feature. By nightfall, their Shermans were established between Points 155 and 170, to the east of the positions held by the Fort Garry Horse. During that night, moreover, the infantry of 1st Canadian Scottish pushed a further 1,200 metres south to seize Hill 175 (the modern Point 174) near Sur le Mont. Despite losing a large number of tanks that day, 2nd Brigade had secured an impressive advance and Simonds saw little reason why this success should not be replicated during the next day's operations.

Meanwhile, by around 1630 hours, the Governor General's Foot Guards and Canadian Grenadier Guards had reassembled most of their dispersed sub-units in the fields south of the Laison between Bout de Haut and Maizières. The two regiments then advanced south-southwest toward Olendon, some 4 km distant, with the British Columbia Regiment following on behind. Around 1645 hours, the Foot Guards reached the woods located around Hill 103 (the modern Point 104, west of the D91 road) and began to consolidate a firm base. Some 15 minutes later, the Grenadiers and the infantry of the Régiment de la Chaudière

TRACTABLE: THE ADVANCE BEYOND THE RIVER LAISON

Soignolles

Va Du sur Nouvres

Its-sur-Laison

Bas d'Eseu

Favières

Estrées-la Campagne

le Val

Maizières

Ernes

Bout du Haut

Rouvres

e Tesson

Montboint

laye

St Quentin la Roche

Olendon

le Breuil

assily

Bernieres d'Ailly

Perrières

So

gy

Epancy

la Queue du Re

Les Monts d'Erames

Ste Anne d Entremont

S¹ Loup

St. Pierre C   et

Station

Aubigny

Versainville

FALAISE

Eraine

la-Mère

▬▬▬▬	Allied front line, 1600 hrs 14 August
▬ ▬ ▬	Allied front line, 2359 hrs 14 August
• • • •	Allied front line, 2359 hrs 15 August
⟶	Infantry movement
⟹	Armoured movement

Base maps:
GSGS 4250 St Pierre sur Dives 7F4, Falaise 7F

0   1
Kilometres

Regina Rifle Regiment	(20)	British Columbia Regiment
Royal Winnipeg Rifles	(21)	Canadian Grenadier Guards
1st Canadian Scottish	(22)	Queen's Own Regiment of Canada
North Nova Scotia Highlanders	(23)	12th Manitoba Dragoons (armoured car screen)
Company, Highland Light Infantry of Canada	(24)	Company, Governor General's Foot Guards
D Company, Highland Light Infantry of Canada	(25)	1st Polish Armoured Division
C Company, Highland Light Infantry of Canada	(26)	1st Polish Armoured Regiment
Stormont, Dundas and Glengarry Highlanders	(27)	10th Polish Motor Battalion
Fort Garry Horse	(28)	Company, 12th SS Panzer Regiment
Duke of York's Royal Canadian Hussars	(29)	Company, I/26th SS Panzergrenadiers
1st Hussars	(30)	12th SS Escort Company
Algonquin Regiment	(31)	Company, III/26th SS Panzergrenadiers
Régiment de la Chaudière	(32)	Company, 12th SS Anti-Tank Battalion
Lincoln and Welland Regiment	(33)	Company, I/25th SS Panzergrenadiers
Argylls of Canada	(34)	Headquarters, 12th SS Panzer Division
North Shore Regiment	(35)	Company, III/12th SS Panzer Artillery
South Alberta Regiment	(36)	Company, 1054th Grenadier Regiment
Lake Superior Regiment	(37)	85th Fusilier Battalion
Governor General's Foot Guards (less one company)	(38)	Battlegroup *Wienecke*

arrived at this location, the latter having advanced down the road from Rouvres. Next, the Argyll and Sutherland Highlanders of Canada and Lincoln and Welland Regiment, each with their attached South Alberta tank squadron, reached Hill 103 around 1715 hours, and finally at 2000 hours the Algonquin Regiment with its attached Shermans arrived at the south-west corner of this ridge. Subsequently, while the other units resumed their advance, the Grenadiers and Foot Guards harboured for the night on Hill 103, supported by the Régiment de la Chaudière.

Around 1800 hours the Lincoln and Wellands and Argylls, each still supported by a South Alberta squadron, advanced from Hill 103 toward Olendon, together with the armour of the British Columbia Regiment. After advancing 2 km to reach the village by 1900 hours, the British Columbia Regiment mounted a left-flank attack from the east, while the other units attacked frontally from the north. They encountered little resistance, and within 30 minutes the Lincoln and Welland Regiment had begun to establish defensive positions within the village. Next, after recce patrols reported that the enemy had recently abandoned Perrières, 2.5 km to the south-east, the Argylls pushed on to capture this village and the nearby Hill 115 before darkness

HISTORY

arrived. Meanwhile, the Algonquin Regiment had moved forward from Hill 103 and skirted round to the east of Olendon. By 2030 hours this battalion, together with elements of the Lake Superior Regiment, had pushed a further 900 metres beyond Olendon to a spot north of Épaney, where they dug in for the night.

As these events unfolded, Allied forces also attempted to secure the offensive's eastern flank. During the late afternoon the North Shore Regiment, with its attached carrier platoon, crossed the Laison using one of the fascine crossings established near Rouvres. Its infantry then marched 3.2 km south-east along the road to Sassy, until they halted, exhausted, 900 metres short of the village. Subsequently, the carrier platoon charged into Sassy, machine guns blazing, and had overwhelmed the small German garrison by 1815 hours, taking a dozen prisoners. Meanwhile, further north, a Canadian armoured car unit mounted patrols along a 3.8-km front that ran from Sassy north up to Ernes, where it linked up with the 51st (Highland) Division. By nightfall, moreover, the latter's flanking operation, having secured le Bû-sur-Rouvres, had advanced 3.2 km further east toward the Laison between Ernes and Ifs-sur-Laison.

By midnight on 14 August, therefore, the Tractable offensive had secured an impressive advance up to 9.3 km deep into the German defences across a maximum frontage of 8.2 km. The Allied front now ran from Quesnay wood to Ouilly-le-Tesson and Hill 160, then progressed from east of Hill 184 through Hill 175 to Olendon, and from there through Perrières, Sassy and Ernes up to Ifs-sur-Laison. For the price of 370 casualties, the II Canadian Corps had successfully broken into the German defensive zone and had taken 560 prisoners. A pleased Simonds now looked forward to his forces repeating these successes the next day by capturing the vital high ground situated north of Falaise.

Simonds' forces, however, made less significant progress on 15 August despite two inexpensively-bought tactical successes – the capture of Hill 184 around noon by the Fort Garry Horse and Royal Winnipeg Rifles, and the successful advance of the 2nd Canadian Division from Clair Tison toward Torp, which consolidated the left flank of Tractable. Elsewhere, however, II Corps units encountered such fierce resistance that their missions either failed, or else were only achieved with high casualties. The Winnipeg Rifles' assault on Soulangy launched that evening, for example, was bloodily repulsed, while the 1st Canadian Scottish attack toward Hill 168 encountered fanatical enemy resistance. However, as described in Stand D4 (*pp. 179–84*), 1st Canadian Scottish – despite lacking intimate tank support – nevertheless fought their way doggedly forward to secure the hill. The Polish Division, committed to the eastern flank to fill the gap previously patrolled by armoured cars, secured a less costly success, advancing 4 km east-southeast that afternoon to secure a bridgehead over the River Dives at Jort. Meanwhile, the Governor General's Foot Guards also successfully advanced 2 km south to approach the north-east fringes of Hill 168, while 2 km further east, the Algonquin, Lincoln and Welland, and Lake Superior Regiments between them captured Épaney.

View from Sur la Route, north of Soulangy, looking north-northwest. During the evening of 15 August the Fort Garry Horse and the Royal Winnipeg Rifles struck south from Hill 184 to secure Soulangy, with elements of the Winnipegs advancing along this road toward the camera. Although these units successfully fought their way into the village, the SS drove them out again; the 50 per cent casualty rate for the Winnipegs' A Company testifies to the ferocity of this action. *(Author)*

Along an axis located between these two actions, moreover, the Canadian Grenadier Guards and British Columbia Regiment successfully by-passed Épaney and then thrust south toward the north-east fringes of Hill 159, the most important of the offensive's objectives. However, given that they lacked infantry support and that their allocated artillery was now out of range, the regiments advanced cautiously toward the summit. As they moved forward, however, intense tank, anti-tank, and artillery

On 14 August, Sergeant Gariepy's 1st Hussars Sherman had an eventful experience with a group of prisoners such as this. During the dash to the Laison, his tank – which had become detached from its unit – suffered wireless problems, jammed machine guns, and a faulty main gun firing mechanism. Despite these problems, Gariepy's crew took 120 German prisoners, whom a nervous Gariepy – with his guns still jammed – marched in front of his tank back to the POW cage at Cauvicourt. Throughout this journey, more German soldiers surrendered, until eventually 352 prisoners were marching in front of the tank. (NAC PA-135954)

fire caught them in the open. This deluge of fire eventually forced the Shermans to withdraw north after incurring heavy casualties – by nightfall the Canadian Grenadier Guards could field just 33 operational tanks. This failure to secure Hill 159 was a key setback for Simonds, all the more so after a tragic misunderstanding occurred late that afternoon. At 1650 hours the Governor General's Foot Guards erroneously reported that its sister regiments had captured Hill 159, news that a relieved Kitching immediately passed on to a delighted Simonds. Later that evening, however, when Simonds learned the truth that 2nd Brigade had actually been driven back from Hill 159, he apparently did not take the news 'at all well'.

Clearly, the momentum initially generated by Tractable had dwindled during 15 August in the face of stiffening resistance. The rapidly developing strategic situation, however, now intervened to save Simonds from having to breathe renewed vigour into his stalled offensive. For, on 15 August, Lt-Gen Crerar ordered the II Corps, once it had captured Falaise, to shift its axis of advance further east. Its two armoured divisions were then to push rapidly toward Trun, where they would link up with the Third US Army to close the Falaise Pocket. Given that, potentially, up to 100,000 German troops might be caught in the pocket, Simonds' II Corps now had the chance to play a crucial role in actions that might seal the fate of the entire German Army deployed in Normandy. These dramatic actions are described in 'Battle Zone Normandy' *Falaise Pocket*.

Consequently, early on 16 August, Simonds issued new orders. The perceptive general realised that the critical sector had already shifted away from Falaise toward Trun, and so he did not wait for Falaise to fall before shifting his main effort eastward. Thus, while his 2nd and 3rd Infantry Divisions continued their drive on Falaise that day, 4th Armoured Division was to abandon its attempt to seize Hill 159. Instead, Simonds ordered the division to cross the River Ante near Damblainville and push south-east along the Falaise–Trun road, alongside the Polish Division, which had advanced from the Dives bridgehead at Jort. Even before Falaise had fallen, therefore, Simonds' eastward shifting of his main effort had reduced the significance of this town's capture. Simonds' new orders also meant that, in effect, by dawn on 16 August he had abandoned Tractable just as its momentum had faltered. Eventually, on 18 August, Simonds' 2nd Division did capture Falaise, but only after it had overwhelmed a suicidal 48-hour-long last stand mounted by 60 *Hitlerjugend* soldiers. The real irony of this achievement was that by the time that Falaise – a town that Simonds had tried so hard since 8 August to dominate – finally fell, the importance of this success had been overshadowed by other battlefield developments.

During the two days of Tractable, II Canadian Corps' numerically superior forces had driven the I SS Corps back to a depth of up to 11 km across a maximum frontage of 12 km. By dawn on 16 August, therefore, the Allied front line now curved south-east from a point north-west of Soulangy through to Hill 168, then ran east-northeast to Perrières, and then arced round to Jort on the Dives, where it turned north toward Vendeuvre. Despite this not insignificant territorial advance, the prematurely abandoned Tractable offensive had struggled to overcome the modest forces arrayed against it and had failed to secure the most important of its objectives, Hill 159. Given this, Tractable – like its 8 August predecessor – has to be considered, at best, an unimpressive partial success, and at worst a disappointing failure.

THE DRIVE ON FALAISE ASSESSED

Although Totalize and Tractable both secured significant territorial gains, neither offensive fully realised Simonds' intent of dominating the key lateral roads that ran through Falaise. This failure is surprising when one considers that Totalize reflected some of the most sophisticated operational art manifested in any Anglo-Canadian offensive mounted in Normandy. In his use of night infiltration by mobile forces, and a second bombing run, Simonds perceptively modified Allied offensive doctrine to emasculate the Germans' most potent defensive capabilities. That neither offensive realised Simonds' intent, however, was due to a combination of factors. First, the firepower-reliant approach sensibly used by Simonds' forces at times proved time-consuming and rather inflexible, and this tempered the offensive momentum that they could generate. In particular, the loss of momentum that occurred on the morning of 8 August during the transition between phases, gave the Germans precious time to recover their badly-shaken cohesion.

With the benefit of hindsight, some historians have concluded that during this period Simonds was unable to surmount the inflexibility inherent in such complex pre-arranged staff planning and scrap this second aerial strike. Consequently, the argument goes, he could not grasp the fleeting opportunity that existed to mount a bold improvised continuation of his break-in operations against a still reeling enemy. Such a view sees insight in Meyer's trenchant critique of Simonds' approach – that it 'transferred the initiative' from 'leading combat elements to timetable acrobats [back at] Headquarters'. Yet crucially, Simonds at this point did not know – probably could not have known – about the weakness of the second German defensive position. Lacking any compelling intelligence to justify scrapping his well-crafted operational plans, Simonds sensibly did what every other commander in 21st Army Group would have done. He continued with the plan, by applying firepower against the seemingly formidable German reserve position. In addition, Meyer's lambaste, quoted above, failed to grasp the operational reality of the Normandy campaign. Allied firepower-reliant operational approaches may have brought tactical sacrifices in terms of flexibility and tempo, but they would eventually take the Allies to a strategic victory over the German Army in the West, and do so at tolerable cost.

The Sherman Firefly, with its potent long-barrelled 17-pounder gun, was the only Anglo-Canadian tank that could stop a Tiger, like Wittmann's, at anything other than extremely short range. In this shot, Sergeant Ginns and Troopers Howard Reed and Lou Capoci, of C Squadron, 1st Northants Yeomanry, load their Firefly on 7 August in preparation for the start of Totalize. *(IWM B8793)*

The second explanation behind the failure of these two operations to achieve Simonds' bold intent, was that some units understandably developed their operations in a cautious and methodical fashion. This manifested itself particularly by units calling artillery down upon large numbers of potential German positions. This understandable approach, which was demonstrated markedly by some armoured units on the afternoon of 8 August, inevitably restricted the tempo of Allied offensive operations. Allied units understandably embraced such cautious approaches, designed to help minimise casualty rates, as their recent combat experiences had given them a healthy regard for the defensive capabilities of the German Army. Such long-range capabilities were only enhanced when the battlefield comprised such easily-defended open terrain as found on the Falaise plain. Furthermore, this Allied perception correctly reflected the wider battlefield reality that by 1944, the defence had – *ceteris paribus* – established a tactical advantage over the offence, as the defensive actions staged by both sides during the previous Normandy battles had demonstrated. Given their long-range killing-power, a few well-concealed German anti-tank guns or a few boldly handled panzers could wreck havoc on advancing Allied units – as the Poles discovered at St-Aignan on 8 August. Any Allied unit that daringly charged off into the unknown, beyond the range of supporting artillery, ran the risk that a swift riposte might inflict appalling losses, as Worthington Force unfortunately discovered.

Yet, probably it was only through such audacity that Simonds' forces could have overwhelmed the desperate German defensive measures they encountered and thus translate tactical achievement into a decisive success. The price of this understandable Allied caution, moreover, was that the Germans gained valuable time to recover the battlefield cohesion that the immediately preceding Allied actions had so recently degraded. Perhaps unsurprisingly, Allied offensive practice in Normandy never fully surmounted the many tensions that arose as a result of the interplay of these various factors. Consequently, during these two offensives, Simonds' forces remained unable to accomplish the significant operational-level success that at various times during these operations – as Meyer correctly perceived – came so tantalisingly close to being realised.

German prisoners are searched after surrendering. Many German soldiers swallowed the Nazi propaganda stories of Allied atrocities. Early on 15 August, for example, North Shore soldiers in Sassy ordered two young German prisoners to dig graves for the bloated bovine corpses that littered the village. Believing that the Canadians were making them dig their own graves prior to execution, the German prisoners began to cry and refused to move! *(NAC PA-162000)*

PART THREE

BATTLEFIELD TOURS

GENERAL TOURING INFORMATION

Normandy is a thriving holiday area, with some beautiful countryside, excellent beaches and very attractive architecture (particularly in the case of religious buildings). It was also, of course, the scene of heavy fighting in 1944, and this has had a considerable impact on the tourist industry. To make the most of your trip, especially if you intend visiting non-battlefield sites, we strongly recommend you purchase one of the general Normandy guidebooks that are commonly available. These include: *Michelin Green Guide: Normandy*; *Thomas Cook Travellers: Normandy*; *The Rough Guide to Brittany and Normandy*; *Lonely Planet: Normandy*.

TRAVEL REQUIREMENTS

First, make sure you have the proper documentation to enter France as a tourist. Citizens of European Union countries, including Great Britain, should not usually require visas, but will need to carry and show their passports. Others should check with the French Embassy in their own country before travelling. British citizens should also fill in and take Form E111 (available from main post offices), which deals with entitlement to medical treatment, and all should consider taking out comprehensive travel insurance. France is part of the Eurozone, and you should also check exchange rates before travelling.

GETTING THERE

The most direct routes from the UK to Lower Normandy are by ferry from Portsmouth to Ouistreham (near Caen), and from Portsmouth or Poole to Cherbourg. Depending on which you choose, and whether you travel by day or night, the crossing takes between four and seven hours. Alternatively, you can sail to Le Havre, Boulogne or Calais and drive the rest of the way. (Travel time from Calais to Caen is about four hours; motorway and bridge

Above: Among the 2,956 graves in the Canadian Military Cemetery near Bretteville-sur Laize are those of soldiers killed during the drive to Falaise, including (in Plot XIX, Row F, Grave 1) that of Lt-Col Worthington who died on 9 August while courageously leading the ill-fated Worthington Force. *(Author)*

Page 109: Mont-Royal Fusilier H. Robichaud patrols along a street in May-sur-Orne on 9 August. The unexpectedly bitter, 18-hour battle for May so ravaged the village that 94 per cent of its houses were destroyed. *(NAC PA-114507)*

tolls may be payable depending on the exact route taken.) Another option is to use the Channel Tunnel. Whichever way you decide to travel, early booking is advised, especially during the summer months.

Although you can of course hire motor vehicles in Normandy, the majority of visitors from the UK or other EU countries will probably take their own. If you do so, you will also need to take: a full driving licence; your vehicle registration document; a certificate of motor insurance valid in France (your insurer will advise on this); spare headlight and indicator bulbs; headlight beam adjusters or tape; a warning triangle; and a sticker or number plate identifying which country the vehicle is registered in. Visitors from elsewhere should consult a motoring organisation in their home country for details of the documents and other items they will require.

Normandy's road system is well developed, although there are still a few choke points, especially around the larger towns during rush hour and in the holiday season. As a general guide, in clear conditions it is possible to drive from Cherbourg to Caen in less than two hours.

ACCOMMODATION

Accommodation in Normandy is plentiful and diverse, from cheap campsites to five star hotels in glorious châteaux. Caen, for example, has over 60 hotels (as well as such other facilities as restaurants and museums). However, early booking is advised if you wish to travel between June and August. Useful contacts include:

French Travel Centre, 178 Piccadilly, London W1V 0AL;
   tel: 0870 830 2000; web: www.raileurope.co.uk
French Tourist Authority, 444 Madison Avenue, New York,
   NY 10022 (other offices in Chicago, Los Angeles and Miami);
   web: www.francetourism.com
Calvados Tourisme, Place du Canada, 14000 Caen;
   tel: +33 (0)2 31 86 53 30; web: www.calvados-tourisme.com
Caen Tourist Information Centre, Hôtel d'Escoville, Place
   St-Pierre, 14000 Caen; tel: +33 (0)2 31 27 14 14;
   web: www.caen.fr/tourisme
Falaise Tourist Information Centre, le Forum, Boulevard de la
   Libération, 14700 Falaise; tel: +33 (0)2 31 90 17 26;
   web: www.otsifalaise.com
Office de Tourisme Intercommunal de Bayeux, Pont Saint-Jean,
   14400 Bayeux; tel: +33 (0)2 31 51 28 28;
   web: www.bayeux-tourism.com
Maison du Tourisme de Cherbourg et du Haut-Cotentin,
   2 Quai Alexandre III, 50100 Cherbourg-Octeville;
   tel: +33 (0)2 33 93 52 02; web: www.ot-cherbourg-cotentin.fr
Gîtes de France, La Maison des Gîtes de France et du Tourisme
   Vert, 59 Rue Saint-Lazare, 75 439 Paris Cedex 09;
   tel: +33 (0)1 49 70 75 75; web: www.gites-de-france.fr

BATTLEFIELD TOURING

Each volume in the 'Battle Zone Normandy' series contains three or more battlefield tours. These are intended to last from a few hours to a full day apiece. Some are best undertaken using motor transport, others should be done on foot, and many involve a mixture of the two. Owing to its excellent infrastructure and relatively gentle topography, Normandy also makes a good location for a cycling holiday; indeed, some of our tours are ideally suited to this method.

In every case the tour author has visited the area concerned recently, so the information presented should be accurate and reasonably up to date. Nevertheless land use, infrastructure and rights of way can change, sometimes at short notice. If you encounter difficulties in following any tour, we would very much like to hear about it, so we can incorporate changes in future editions. Your comments should be sent to the publisher at the address provided at the front of this book.

South Saskatchewan soldiers relax on 8 August after capturing Rocquancourt the previous night. Lance-Corporal M.H. Krushelinski bathes his feet while Private J.A. Balogh (*centre*) and Lance-Corporal P. Kostyk look on. *(NAC PA-129136)*

To derive maximum value and enjoyment from the tours, we suggest you equip yourself with the following items:

- Appropriate maps. European road atlases can be purchased from a wide range of locations outside France. However, for navigation within Normandy, the French Institut Géographique National (IGN) produces maps at a variety of scales (www.ign.fr). The 1:100,000 series ('Top 100') is particularly useful when driving over larger distances; sheet 06 (Caen – Cherbourg) covers most of the invasion area. For pinpointing locations precisely, the current IGN 1:25,000 Série Bleue is best (extracts from this series are used for the tour maps in this book). These can be purchased in many places across Normandy. They can also be ordered in the UK from some bookshops, or from specialist dealers such as the Hereford Map Centre, 24–25 Church Street, Hereford HR1 2LR; tel: 01432 266322; web: <www.themapcentre.com>. Allow at least a fortnight's notice, although some maps may be in stock.

- Lightweight waterproof clothing and robust footwear are essential, especially for touring in the countryside.
- Take a compass, provided you know how to use one!
- A camera and spare films/memory cards.
- A notebook to record what you have photographed.
- A French dictionary and/or phrasebook. (English is widely spoken in the coastal area, but is much less common inland.)
- Food and drink. Although you are never very far in Normandy from a shop, restaurant or *tabac*, many of the tours do not pass directly by such facilities. It is therefore sensible to take some light refreshment with you.
- Binoculars. Most officers and some other ranks carried binoculars in 1944. Taking a pair adds a surprising amount of verisimilitude to the touring experience.

Captured near Tilly-la-Campagne on 8 August, these prisoners hail from the German 89th Infantry Division, which manned a 9,000-metre sector of the front that stretched from May-sur-Orne to la Hogue. *(NAC PA-116509)*

SOME DO'S AND DON'TS

Battlefield touring can be an extremely interesting and even emotional experience, especially if you have read something about the battles beforehand. In addition, it is fair to say that residents of Normandy are used to visitors, among them battlefield tourers, and generally will do their best to help if you encounter problems. However, many of the tours in the 'Battle Zone Normandy' series are off the beaten track, and you can expect some puzzled looks from the locals, especially inland. In all cases we have tried to ensure that tours are on public land, or viewable from public rights of way. However, in the unlikely event that you are asked to leave a site, do so immediately and by the most direct route.

In addition: **Never remove 'souvenirs' from the battlefields.** Even today it is not unknown for farmers to turn up relics of the 1944 fighting. Taking these without permission may not only be illegal, but can be extremely dangerous. It also ruins the site for genuine battlefield archaeologists. Anyone returning from France should also remember customs regulations on the import of weapons and ammunition of any kind.

Be especially careful when investigating fortifications. Some of the more frequently-visited sites are well preserved, and several of them have excellent museums. However, both along the coast and inland there are numerous positions that have been left to decay, and which carry risks for the unwary. In particular, remember that many of these places were the scenes of heavy fighting or subsequent demolitions, which may have caused severe (and sometimes invisible) structural damage. Coastal erosion has also undermined the foundations of a number of shoreline defences. Under no circumstances should underground bunkers, chambers and tunnels be entered, and care should always be taken when examining above-ground structures. If in any doubt, stay away.

Beware of hunting (shooting) areas (signposted *Chasse Gardée*). Do not enter these, even if they offer a short cut to your destination. Similarly, Normandy contains a number of restricted areas (military facilities and wildlife reserves), which should be avoided. Watch out, too, for temporary footpath closures, especially along sections of coastal cliffs.

If using a motor vehicle, keep your eyes on the road. There are many places to park, even on minor routes, and it is always better to turn round and retrace your path than to cause an accident. In rural areas avoid blocking entrances and driving along farm tracks; again, it is better to walk a few hundred metres than to cause damage and offence.

In addition, three points specific to this volume ought to be raised. First, when the principal reconnaissance for this book was done – in mid-August, close to the seasonal conditions in which these battles were fought – most of the local fields had been harvested. The advantage of conducting the tour when the fields have been harvested is that the tourer enjoys a better field of vision. However, the tourer seeking maximum authenticity should note that back in August 1944 many of the fields had not been harvested due to the war, and that the crops would have stood up to two metres tall. The presence of unharvested crops would have given the foot soldier a different perspective on this landscape than the one obtained by the author.

The author standing by some tall unharvested crops – fields such as this would have altered considerably the foot soldiers' perception of the battlefield. *(Author)*

Second, these tours have followed as closely as possible the actual routes taken by the units whose actions they examine, traversing where necessary narrow and undulating grassy tracks. The author successfully followed all these tracks in an ordinary car when the ground conditions were good; nevertheless, drivers should proceed very cautiously along these routes to avoid damaging their vehicles. If tours are attempted when the weather is wet and/or the ground soft, it is recommended that tourers avoid using these grassy tracks. Where possible, this guide has indicated alternative routes that follow tarmac roads to get the tourer close to the stands; these should be used if the conditions are unsuitable for off-road travel.

Finally, it should be noted that, at the time of writing, the N158 (the main Caen–Falaise road) was in the middle of an extensive reconstruction scheme that may not be shown on the edition of the map you possess. The former N158 intersections at Lorguichon and les Fresnots (near Quesnay) no longer exist;

drivers can only join or exit the N158 in this area at the Cormelles-le-Royal, la Guingette, la Jalousie, Haut Mesnil, Langannerie, Potigny, and Soulangy intersections.

Those undertaking the tours in this book will find invaluable the following IGN Série Bleue maps: *1512 E (Caen)* which shows how to get onto the N158 road; *1513 E (Thury-Harcourt)*, which covers the May-sur-Orne area; the essential *1613 O (Bretteville-sur-Laize)* which covers most of the Totalize battlefield and the northern part of Tractable; *1614 O (Falaise)* and *1614 E (Morteaux-Couliboeuf)*, which between them cover the southern part of the Tractable battlefield; and finally *1613 E (Mézidon-Canon)*, which covers the eastern flank of Tractable.

The grave in the Polish Military Cemetery of a Jewish soldier of the 1st Polish Armoured Division killed on 9 August. *(Author)*

Tourers may also feel it appropriate to visit the two Allied war cemeteries that contain the graves of servicemen killed during these operations. Both the Canadian Military Cemetery at Bretteville-sur-Laize and the Polish Military Cemetery at Urville–Langannerie are located close to the N158, at sites north of Cintheaux and north-northwest of Langannerie respectively.

Another issue that tourers might wish to consider is that shops are rare in this area, so it might be sensible to take packed lunches. Those eating-places that do exist in the smaller communities include: the *Café le Saint Patrick* (at the St-André crossroads); the two bar/tabacs *Au rendez-vous des Sportifs* (on the D80 at le Haut Bosq near St-Aignan, and in Bourguébus); the bar/tabac in Hubert-Folie; *le Triangle Bar-Brasserie* in Rouvres; and *la Relais* restaurant (near the former N158 intersection at Lorguichon, which can now only be reached via the D41). In addition, St-André, Bretteville-sur-Laize, Caen, Falaise, Mondeville and Potigny offer a variable range of shops and eating-places.

Given the range of accommodation and facilities available in Caen, plus its easy access to these battlefields, the directions given in this work assumes that tourers will stay in Caen. However, Falaise is a suitable alternative base for those wishing to explore these battlefields as the N158 makes it straightforward to move between these two centres.

For those tourers wishing to spend time in other ways, the Caen area offers a range of activities. These activities include (in Caen itself) the Caen Memorial Museum, the Museum of Fine Arts, the 11th century Men's and Ladies' Abbeys, the 150-minute boat trip down the Caen Canal to Ouistreham via Pegasus Bridge, the la Prairie children's activity centre (for 4–16 year olds), and the de la Grâce de Dieu swimming pool. Outside Caen, such activities include the 11th century Château Creully (17 km north-west of Caen), the Ancient Roman Archaeological Museum (9 km south-west of Caen), the bowling alley in Mondeville, Château Vendeuvre and its gardens (11 km north-east of Falaise), and in Falaise itself the 11th century castle, the August 1944 museum, and the mechanical figure museum.

Contact Details

August 1944 Museum, Chemin des Roches, 14700 Falaise; tel: +33 (0)2 31 90 37 19

Automates Avenue Mechanical Figure Museum, Boulevard de la Libération, 14700 Falaise; tel: + 33 (0)2 31 90 02 43; email: automates@mail.cpod.fr

Bateau l'Hastings Boat Trips, (Caen – Pegasus Bridge – Ouistreham), Quai Vendeuvre, BP 3052, 14018 Caen, Cedex 2; tel: +33 (0)2 31 34 00 00; web: www.bateau-hasting.com

Bowling du Calvados, 10-Pin Bowling Alley, 6 Rue Charles Coulomb, Mondeville; tel: +33 (0)2 31 82 53 58

Creully Château, Creully; tel: + 33 (0)2 31 80 18 65

Falaise Castle, 14700 Falaise; tel: +33 (0)2 31 41 61 69; email: chateau.falaise@wanadoo.fr

La Prairie Children's Activity Centre, 11 Avenue Sorel, 14000 Caen; tel: +33 (0)2 31 85 25 16; web: www.la-prairie.com

Caen Museum of Fine Arts, Le Château, 14000 Caen; tel: + 33 (0)2 31 30 47 70; web: www.ville-caen.fr/mba

Swimming Pool de la Grâce de Dieu, 20 Avenue Père Charles de Foucauld, 14000 Caen; tel: +33 (0)2 31 52 19 78

Caen Memorial Museum, Esplanade Dwight Eisenhower, BP 6261, 14066 Caen, Cedex 4; tel: +33 (0)2 31 06 06 44; web: www.memorial-caen.fr

Vendeuvre Château and Gardens, 14170 Vendeuvre; tel: +33 (0)2 31 40 93 83; web: www.vendeuvre.com

Vieux-la-Romaine Roman Archaeological Museum, 13 Chemin Hauseé, 14930 Vieux; tel: + 33 (0)2 31 71 10 20; email: vieuxlaroamine@cg14.fr

TOUR A

'TOTALIZE' – THE MOBILE COLUMN ASSAULT

OBJECTIVE: This tour explores the deep and rapid break-in battle mounted by the Allied mobile columns during the night of 7/8 August 1944.

DURATION/SUITABILITY: This tour will take more than half a day by car. It is not suitable as a walking tour, because of the distance involved, but is suitable for fit cyclists (taking a full day), although some may wish to find an alternative route that avoids using the N158. Most stands are accessible by car but tourers with mobility difficuties may find the considerable amount of off-road travel uncomfortable. The tour map will help plan alternative routes on tarmac roads. Stand A3 requires climbing a steep embankment up to the bridge and is not accessible for those with mobility difficulties.

View of Stand A1 taken from just east of the bend in the D89 looking west. In the left foreground is the wall of Troteval Farm, while visible on the horizon is Beauvoir Farm. The stand is on the right-hand side of the road, just beyond the telegraph post. *(Author)*

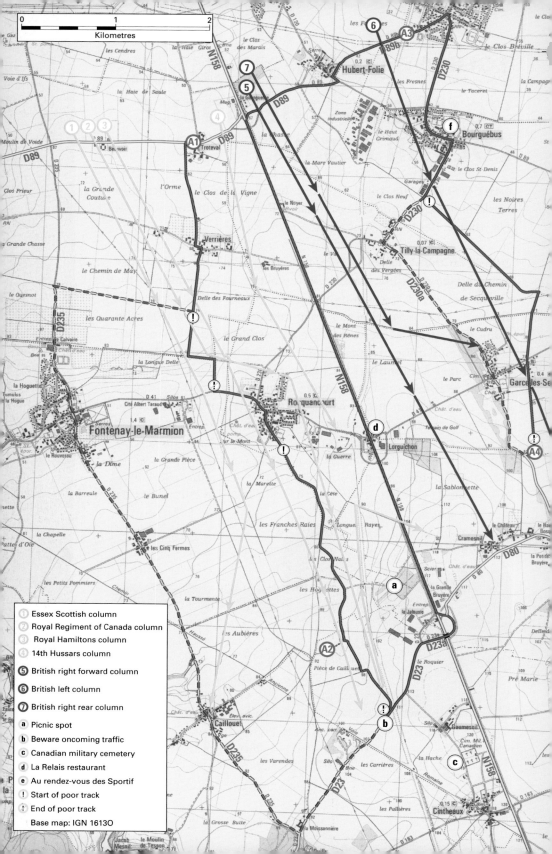

①	Essex Scottish column
②	Royal Regiment of Canada column
③	Royal Hamiltons column
④	14th Hussars column
⑤	British right forward column
⑥	British left column
⑦	British right rear column
a	Picnic spot
b	Beware oncoming traffic
c	Canadian military cemetery
d	La Relais restaurant
e	Au rendez-vous des Sportif
!	Start of poor track
!	End of poor track
	Base map: IGN 1613O

Stand A1: The Canadian Columns' Start Line

DIRECTIONS: Drive south from Caen on the N158 to la Guingette and head west on the D89 for 600 metres. Park near Troteval Farm and walk west past the farm's tall stone wall.

ORIENTATION: Stand just north of the D89 to the west of the farm's stone wall and face south along the axis of the road that runs up the slopes of the Verrières Ridge to the hamlet of the same name, 1.2 km distant. To the front-right are the open fields of l'Orme and la Grand Couture, while 950 metres to the right (west) are the red-roofed cream-walled buildings of Beauvoir Farm. To the north are visible the southern outskirts of Caen.

THE ACTION: In 1944 this road marked the start line for the western (Canadian) sector of Totalize, including the forming-up points for all four Canadian mobile columns. During the late evening of 7 August the 14th Hussars column formed up on the north side of this road 400 metres east of this stand, just out of sight round the bend. Simultaneously, the remaining three columns assembled close together north of the road 100 metres west of Beauvoir Farm (1 km to the west of this stand). This triple formation fielded the Essex Scottish column furthest west, the Royal Regiment of Canada in the centre, and the Royal Hamiltons to the east, closest to this stand. The western column was to capture Caillouet, the centre column Hill 122, and the eastern column Gaumesnil and the quarry 1.1 km south-west of this hamlet. The three were to advance 5.3 km south-southeast to Stand A2 – the fields of Pièce de Caillouet – where their infantry would debus from their carriers and assault their objectives.

From 2330 hours – in the face of light German fire – these three columns rumbled south-southeast past Beauvoir Farm across the fields of l'Orme and la Grand Couture toward the western edge of the orchards by Verrières (1.3 km south of this stand). Around 2345 hours, having reached that village, the columns picked up the rear edge of the creeping barrage that Allied field artillery had just begun to deliver. Subsequently, the three columns – following the barrage as it rolled deeper into the German lines – rumbled through the darkness at 11 km/hr, heading south-southeast towards the fields of Delle des Fourneaux and le Grand Clos. At this point the columns crossed the track south from Verrières (down which this tour will pass) around Point 74, near where the modern pylons cross over it.

As the 600 vehicles fielded by these columns advanced over the tinder-dry ground, however, they threw up dense dust clouds. Soon this dust had so thickened the night's darkness that this overwhelmed Allied efforts to provide the columns with guidance from diffused searchlights and tracer rounds. Not surprisingly, navigation soon became problematic and consequently the columns fragmented as they advanced. This appalling visibility caused the formation of the Essex Scottish column in particular to collapse as it advanced across the eastern fringes of le Chemin de May. Despite this increasing fragmentation, the three columns struggled on, and eventually passed beyond the view obtainable at this stand, crossing le Grand Clos to close on Rocquancourt.

View taken from Point 62 (400 metres south of Stand A1) looking west-northwest across the fields of la Grande Couture toward Beauvoir Farm. From its assembly area – 100 metres west-northwest of the farm– the Canadian triple column formation advanced south-southeast across this area as shown. (Author)

Stand A2: The Canadian Columns' Debus Area

DIRECTIONS: From Stand A1, rejoin the D89 west for 120 metres, then turn left into a narrow road heading south for 1.2 km. Turn left (east) through Verrières for 30 metres, then turn right before the stone chapel (note the commemorative plaque on the wall) onto a grass track heading cautiously south for 700 metres to Point 74, where a gravel track joins from the left/west.

As Canadian tank units advanced across the Normandy fields during Totalize, they threw up dense clouds of dust that caused them immense command and control problems. At one point, the commander of one of the Essex Scottish column's spearhead flail tanks realised to his horror that he could not see the end of the jib at the front of his vehicle, let alone any nearby tanks. *(NAC PA-128954)*

To continue on the standard route beyond Point 74 (the grass track south of Point 74 deteriorates significantly – for an easier route on roads, follow the alternative directions), head straight on down the track for 500 metres, then turn left at Point 72 and continue east for 300 metres. Turn right at Point 67 and go south for 400 metres, then left at Point 69 onto the D41. Drive east-southeast for 800 metres into Rocquancourt. By the church, turn right at the T-junction before the *mairie*, continue south for 120 metres. then take the left fork heading south-east for 170 metres. Go straight on at the crossroads heading south-southeast for 1.8 km (this road becomes first a gravel track then a grass track) until another grass track joins from the left (east) at les Hoguettes (you can make an optional picnic detour 550 metres east down this track past Point 96 to a pleasant clearing in a copse). From les Hoguettes continue south-southeast for 600 metres to Point 94 (where the track you are on bends left then sharply right just after a further grass track joins from the right). Park here, and walk along the track to the right (west) for 150 metres until a slight rise provides a good field of vision.

ALTERNATIVE ROUTE: At Point 74, turn right onto a gravel track and head west for 1.3 km. Turn left/south onto the D235 for 5.6 km, then left onto the D23 (north-east of Bretteville-sur-Laize) heading north-east for 2 km. Turn left onto a grass track before the road crosses the railway line by Point 111, then park and walk 1 km north-northwest up the grass track until Stand A2 is reached by Point 94.

The author looking south across the fields of Pièce de Caillouet from the track junction by Point 94. The stand is 150 metres down the track that runs right (west) past the author, at the crest of a slight rise. *(Author)*

ORIENTATION: Stand facing south looking across the open fields of Pièce de Caillouet toward the silo visible on the horizon (1.5 km away just south of les Carrières quarry). Visible 1.3 km to the front-right (south-west) is Caillouet, with its white domed grain silo, while 1.1 km to the front-left is the bridge carrying the D23 over the former iron-ore railway line by Point 111. Finally, to the rear-right Fontenay-le-Marmion and Rocquancourt can be seen, 3.5 km north-west and 2.5 km north-northwest respectively.

THE ACTION: From 0100 hours on 8 August, the three Canadian columns began to close on Rocquancourt in the face of sporadic fire. The dispersed Essex Scottish column approached the eastern fringes of la Longue Delle, 1.2 km west-northwest of the village (3.2 km to the right-rear of this stand). Meanwhile, the eastern (Royal Hamiltons) column, having crossed le Grand Clos, approached Rocquancourt from the north-northwest down what is now the D230. Finally, the disorientated central (Royal Regiment) column – less its already fragmented B Company – failed to pass west of the village across the eastern fringes of Sur le Mont as planned; instead the force blundered into the Royal Hamiltons column as it rumbled south through the northern fringes of Rocquancourt, creating a lengthy traffic jam. The Royal Regiment group only extricated itself from this jam by abandoning its planned route of advance with a detour to the east of Rocquancourt. Consequently, the Royal Regiment and Royal Hamiltons columns had, in effect, swapped their original positions within the triple formation so that the former now moved along the eastern axis and the Royal Hamiltons the central route.

View taken from south of Rocquancourt looking south-east along the track that the Royal Regiment and Royal Hamilton columns followed on their advance to the debus point at Pièce de Caillouet (Stand A2). *(Author)*

Having passed south of Rocquancourt by 0230 hours, the two columns continued south-southeast toward this stand (their debus area). The Royal Regiment column advanced south-east along the track from Rocquancourt down to the debus area – along which this tour travelled – until at 0330 hours it reached Pièce de Caillouet. Some minutes behind this force, the Royal Hamiltons column advanced south-southeast down this same track, although some of its elements crossed the fields of la Cète and Longues Rayes along an axis 150 metres further east. Meanwhile, the dispersed Essex Scottish column remained stalled around la Longue Delle and Sur le Mont, after sustained anti-tank fire had knocked out its leading vehicles, throwing the remainder into even greater confusion.

View taken from Point 69 on the D41 road (450 metres north-west of Rocquancourt) looking south across the fields of Sur le Mont. The Essex Scottish column only determined its position at 0500 hours when one of its officers entered a nearby village and was told by South Saskatchewan infantrymen that he was in Rocquancourt. *(Author)*

By around 0400 hours the elements of the Royal Regiment column that had managed to reach the debus area (positioned to the front of this stand) moved off with their infantry still embussed in carriers. The column headed 500 metres north up the western side of the nearby iron-ore railway embankment (visible to the left rear) to the spot south of Point 96 where a gap existed in the embankment – through which this tour's picnic detour route passed. The force had intended to pass through this gap before striking east to secure its objective, Hill 122, but failed to locate it in the darkness. Consequently, the column had to detour around the northern tip of the embankment at Point 90, before eventually assembling east of the embankment in the fields of Longues Rayes, 150 metres south-west of Point 90. This unexpected development forced the column commander rapidly to improvise a new plan, as he knew his force would incur greater casualties if it attacked in daylight, which was then approaching. Instead of striking north-east from Point 96 as planned, the column's carriers would thrust 800 metres east from Point 90 across the main Caen–Falaise road to seize Hill 122, while the Shermans provided fire support from the rear.

At 0600 hours, ten of the column's 12 remaining Priests, carrying the troops of A and D Companies, stormed uphill through the emerging daylight onto the summit, where they disgorged their soldiers. During the next 25 minutes, the infantry secured the hill after encountering only light German small-arms fire. Subsequently, the rest of the column arrived and frantically dug defensive positions, anticipating that the Germans would soon attempt to regain this vital high ground. At 0900 hours this fear was realised, when a mixed German tank and infantry force counter-attacked north along the main Caen–Falaise road. Despite encountering furious Canadian fire, one Panther penetrated the column's defensive perimeter before being knocked out. Over the next hour the bloody battle raged on, with acrid filth polluting the crisp morning air from the wrecks of four panzers and six Canadian vehicles, but eventually the defenders drove the surviving German forces back south in disarray; the key objective of Hill 122 had been secured.

View taken from east of the N158 on the western edge of the summit of Hill 122 looking north-west across the fields of Longues Rayes. Beyond, the iron-ore railway embankment runs from left to right up to Point 90. (*Author*)

To ensure that his infantry kept up with the tanks, Simonds arranged for surplus Priest self-propelled guns to be converted into infantry carriers such as these. *(TTM 2292/E2)*

Meanwhile, back at 0530 hours the debussed infantry of the Royal Hamiltons column advanced south across the exposed fields – visible to the front of this stand – toward les Carrieres quarry, 900 metres away. Although the infantry pushed 500 metres toward their objective, fierce German fire then pinned them down, forcing them, once daylight had emerged, to establish a defensive perimeter 400 metres south of this stand.

While these events unfolded, the disorientated Essex Scottish column remained static in the eastern fringes of la Longue Delle, 3.2 km north-northwest of this stand, where it reassembled its dispersed elements in readiness to resume the attack on Caillouet. Next, at 0845 hours, the column – supported by elements of the 14th Hussars – advanced south across the fields of Sur le Mont and la Marette along an axis 900 metres west of the track from Rocquancourt down to this stand. The column soon reached the top of the slight crest near Point 84, north of les Aubieres, 1.1 km west-northwest of this stand.

At this point, however, the column halted after spotting four panzers dug-in in front of Caillouet. When the column commander invited the leader of the supporting towed 17-pounder anti-tank gun troop to engage them, he allegedly declined on the grounds that this would endanger his weapons. Consequently, it was not until 1100 hours – after the tanks had withdrawn – that the column was ready to assault Caillouet. As supporting artillery, tank and Priest infantry carrier firepower suppressed the defences, the column's remaining carriers boldly carried the infantry all the way into the village, contrary to normal practice. Here, the men debussed and gradually fought their way into the village in the face of bitter resistance that included *Nebelwerfer* fire. Eventually the surviving German soldiers began to withdraw, fleeing west through the defile north-west of the village. Thus, by noon, the column had secured Caillouet and the surrounding area.

Stand A3: The Left British Column's Start Line

DIRECTIONS: From the Stand A2 parking spot, continue on the grass track south-southeast through Pièce de Caillouet for 600 metres, then turn left onto the D23 (beware of fast-moving on-coming traffic appearing over the crest ahead) for 750 metres. Take the right fork onto the D23a, heading east for 400 metres (passing over the N158), then north-northwest for 250 metres. Take the left fork west for 40 metres, then turn right on the slip road (at la Jalousie intersection) to join the N158 north for 5.4 km. Leave the N158 at la Guingette intersection and continue east-northeast on the D89 for 800 metres. Turn left into Hubert-Folie and take the right fork by church onto the D89b. Drive on east-northeast (signposted Soliers) for 800 metres; 100 metres after passing under a rail bridge, park in the gravel area on the right. Walk back to, and up onto, the bridge.

ORIENTATION: Stand on the southern end of the bridge facing south-southwest along the axis of the disused railway embankment. Some 900 metres to the front-left are visible the buildings in Bourguébus, including the distinctive post-war church. To the front-right can be seen Hubert-Folie (800 metres south-southwest along the D89b), and to the south-west the industrial park near le Haut Grimaud, 900 metres distant. To the rear-left and rear-right are visible the villages of Soliers and Bras.

View taken from Stand A3 looking south-west along the embankment of the former iron-ore railway line toward Bourguébus, 800 metres away, and the bridge over the railway by Point 54. Some 500 metres from the camera the embankment peters out and re-emerges 100 metres further south. The left British column advanced from the right of this photo through this gap, before heading off over the horizon where the post-war houses by the bridge are now situated. *(Author)*

THE ACTION: By 2315 hours on 7 August, Lt-Col Forster's left British column had assembled on its start line just north of the Hubert-Folie–Soliers road, 300 metres west of this stand (where the pylons cross the road). The column comprised the tanks of Forster's 1st Northants Yeomanry, the embussed infantry of Lt-Col John Hopwood's 1st Black Watch, plus support that included a troop of flail tanks. The column was to advance 6.3 km south-southeast, by-passing the German positions in Tilly, to capture St-Aignan-de-Cramesnil and the adjacent wooded high ground. At 2330 hours the column began to advance, and soon passed east of the railway via the gap in the embankment at les Fresnes (500 metres south-southwest of this stand). Then, at 2345 hours, the column approached the rear edge of the rolling artillery barrage as it landed on the area south of Bourguébus. Next, however, as the barrage rolled south, the column's leading flail tanks struggled to cross several sunken lanes located south-southwest of Bourguébus, and consequently the column's advance fell behind that of the barrage. Despite Forster's concern that his command might now suffer heavier casualties, having lost the barrage's suppressive effect on the Germans, he nevertheless continued to drive his force forward. Subsequently, the column advanced south-southeast beyond Bourguébus across the fields of le Clos Neuf, where it was fired on from Tilly. At this point the column disappeared from the view today obtainable at this stand.

View from Stand A3 looking south-west along the D89 road toward Hubert-Folie. The left British column assembled in the field to the north (*right*) of this road. During the previous hour, the column had moved south to this start line along routes which engineers had illuminated with amber lights. (*Author*)

Stand A4: The Left British Column's Assault on St-Aignan-de-Cramesnil

DIRECTIONS: Continue north-east along the D89b for 300 metres into Soliers and turn right at the mini-roundabout onto the D230 (signposted Bourguébus). Drive on south-southeast then south-southwest for 1.3 km. Go straight on at the mini-roundabout by Point 42 (note the remains of the Bourguébus church destroyed in 1944), continuing south then south-east for 650 metres. Turn right by the new church (signposted Tilly-la-Campagne), continue south-southwest for 800 metres, then (after passing a building on the left and garages on the right) turn left onto a grass track heading south-east for 1.7 km through Delle du Chemin de Secqueville. Next, turn right onto another grass track heading south for 800 metres; go straight on at the crossroads by Point 79 (400 metres east of Garcelles-Secqueville) onto a road (Chemin des Bruyères) that becomes a grass track. Continue south for 1 km and park where the track bends right sharply (170 metres north-east of Point 92).

ALTERNATIVE ROUTE: Rather than turn left onto the grass track after the garages, stay on the road for 700 metres to Tilly, then turn left onto the D230a, heading south-southeast for 2 km. Go straight on at the crossroads in Garcelles-Sequeville into a narrow lane. Continue south for 1 km and park where a grass track joins from the left by Point 92. Walk to Stand A4.

ORIENTATION: Stand facing south-east looking across the fields toward the church spire at St-Aignan, 1.1 km away. On the left (east-northeast) are the open fields of le Castelet, across which in 1944 a tall tree-hedge ran. To the south and north-west respectively can be seen the road and the narrow wooded strip that runs south-southeast from Garcelles-Sequeville to le Haut du Bosq, 500 metres west of St-Aignan.

View from Point 92 looking north-east toward Stand A4 (by the bend 170 metres away). Beyond are the fields of le Castelet, across which in 1944 a tree-hedge ran past the tall pole to what is now the D229a road. The left British column found gaps in the hedge made by German tanks and exploited this good fortune by not debussing the infantry at the hedge as planned. *(Author)*

THE ACTION: After moving through the dust-thickened darkness across le Clos Neuf around 0040 hours on 8 August, Forster's column subsequently rumbled 1.5 km south-southeast across the fields of Delle du Chemin de Secqueville (through which this tour has passed). In the face of intermittent German fire, the column's increasingly dispersed vehicles then continued south-southeast, passing through the crossroads at Point 79

(1.1 km north of this stand) to by-pass Garcelles-Sequeville. The 200-vehicle formation then headed south-east, cutting across to the east of the track from Point 79 to this stand (along which this tour has travelled) to approach the fields of le Castelet.

View of St-Aignan church from Stand A4 by the now removed hedge-line at le Castelet. As the left British column pushed south toward the village, the Germans fought back by inaccurately mortaring the general area, suggesting that in the dust-reinforced gloom they had not determined the column's precise location. *(Author)*

Around 0240 hours, the lead (navigator's) vehicle halted the column at its debus area – the now cleared tree-hedge line that in 1944 ran east from Point 92 across le Castelet to Point 91 on what is now the D229a road. The Allies had selected this thick hedge as the debus area because they believed that the column's vehicles could not get through it and that the feature offered the carriers some protection from German fire once the troops had debussed. Despite losing the protection afforded by the rolling barrage, the column up to then had avoided serious casualties, losing just two Priest infantry carriers *en route*. At 0325 hours, the column's unexpected discovery of gaps in the hedge enabled its vehicles to advance a further 800 metres south-southeast to the hedge 300 metres north of St-Aignan, while supporting artillery fire descended on the village. As this strike continued, two Sherman squadrons pushed through gaps in this second hedge and engaged targets in St-Aignan, along the nearby hedge lines, and in the woods north of le Haut Bosq. Meanwhile, along this second hedge, two infantry companies debussed from their Priests, in readiness to assault the village.

Next, at 0345 hours, after the artillery had ceased, the infantry stormed the village, while frantic Sherman fire strove to suppress any defenders. As the infantry fought themselves into the village, they met fierce German resistance that inflicted several dozen casualties. Subsequently, however, the Germans executed a gradual fighting withdrawal to the south, and thus the column secured the village within the hour, having taken 40 prisoners in the process. During the next few hours the column established firm defensive positions around St-Aignan despite the dense mist that had descended on the area. Overall, the left British column had secured an impressive 6.3-km penetration of the German line at the tolerable price of 11 killed and 58 wounded or missing.

ENDING THE TOUR: From Stand A4, continue south-west on the grass track for 170 metres and turn left/south-east for 950 metres. Turn right at le Haut Bosq, for 100 metres, then right onto the D80 for 250 metres. Take the left-hand fork by Point 106 to continue on the D80 and join the N158 at la Jalousie intersection and return to Caen.

TOUR B

'TOTALIZE' – THE INFANTRY ASSAULT

OBJECTIVE: This tour explores the two key Allied foot infantry actions mounted during the night of 7/8 August: the Canadian assault on May-sur-Orne and the British attack on Tilly-la-Campagne.

DURATION/SUITABILITY: This tour will take half a day by car. It is suitable for cyclists (probably taking over half a day). but not as a walking tour, because of the substantial distance involved. Those with mobility difficulties may find the short piece of off-road travel between Stands B4 and B5 very uncomfortable.

a Café St-Patrick
b New mini-roundabout
c Triple silo structure
d Mairie gardens monuments
e Au rendez-vous des Sportif
f No access to N158
g La Relais restaurant
! Start of poor track
? End of poor track

Base maps: IGN 1513E,
IGN 1613O

Kilometres
0   1   2

VERRIÈRES RIDGE
les Quarante Acres

The tour map will help plan alternative routes that use tarmac roads. Reaching Stand B3 requires a walk of about 130 metres across rough scrub land.

Stand B1: The Attack on May-sur-Orne

DIRECTIONS: Drive south from Caen on the N158 to the Cormelles-le-Royal intersection. Turn right/west on the N814 for 1.8 km, then left/south onto the D562 for 900 metres (towards St-Martin-de-Fontenay) until you reach a wooded hill on the left. Turn left past the large building, heading east-northeast up a rutted track for 100 metres, then dog-leg back to the left and park in the gravel area.

ORIENTATION: Stand by the monument looking south along the D562 as it descends toward St-André-sur-Orne, St-Martin-de-Fontenay, and beyond to May-sur-Orne. Then walk 250 metres east-northeast up the track and face east-southeast toward Beauvoir Farm. You are on Hill 67, from where the Allies could observe the western flank of Totalize. Visible to the southeast are the northern slopes of the Verrières Ridge. Also visible 2.5 km away to the south-southwest is the distinctive triple silo structure by the ravine north-west of May-sur-Orne.

The monument at Stand B1 commemorates the actions fought nearby during Operations 'Goodwood' (18–20 July) and 'Spring' (25–26 July). *(Author)*

THE ACTION: The 2nd Canadian Division's plan envisaged that, during the night of 7/8 August, as its columns advanced, an infantry battalion of 6th Brigade would secure the vulnerable right (western) flank that bordered the River Orne. Lt-Col Gauvreau's Les Fusiliers Mont-Royal were to strike south down the road from St-André and St-Martin to capture May-sur-Orne after the village had been hit by Allied strategic bombers. The Fusiliers' front that night ran east from the Orne around le Petit Moulin to what is now the north of la Cité de la Mine, and thence north-east towards Beauvoir Farm. Facing the Fusiliers were elements of the 1st Battalion of *Oberst* (Colonel) Roesler's 1056th Grenadier Regiment, from 89th Division. The battalion's front ran for 2.7 km from Percouville to May, and thence 2.8 km across the Verrières Ridge to just north of Verrières.

As the Fusiliers' front line was only 1.3 km north of the intended Allied strategic bombing strike on May, Gauvreau remained concerned that friendly-fire casualties might occur if any bombs dropped short. To this end, II Corps had established a safety line – north of which the bombers were not to drop their payloads – that ran through Hill 67. At 2230 hours on 7 August, however, Gauvreau only withdrew his forces 500 metres to the St-André crossroads, a full 1.1 km south of this safety line; presumably he preferred to risk some friendly-fire casualties rather than have his soldiers advance, while under German fire, 1.6 km across ground that they had voluntarily given up. Around 2255 hours, however, as the Fusiliers reached this crossroads, a German artillery barrage inflicted heavy casualties on the battalion, including many injuries caused by shrapnel that ricocheted off the thick walls of the nearby cottages. With the unit now depleted and its soldiers dazed, the Fusiliers' operation could scarcely have got off to a less auspicious start.

View taken from Stand B1 looking south-east across the fields of le Moulin de Voide. In 1944 this lane formed the Canadian start line for Totalize. *(Author)*

BATTLEFIELD TOURS

A few minutes later, at 2300 hours, the lead Lancasters dropped their bombs on targets in and around May, which Allied artillery had identified with coloured smoke rounds. The intense clouds of dust generated by the initial bombing runs, however, so reduced visibility over the target that the rear squadrons either abandoned their missions rather than risk friendly-fire accidents or else inaccurately dropped their bombs blind. Given this bombing support and the outflanking advance of the columns, Simonds had expected the Fusiliers to encounter only weak opposition in May. Yet after this imperfect bombing strike, the subsequent Fusilier attacks on May – as the next two stands describe – encountered more determined resistance than anyone on the Allied side had ever anticipated.

View taken from the D562 road looking south at the St-André crossroads. At 2255 hours on 7 August, an unknown German officer heard the massed Allied bombers approaching. He deduced that May was about to be bombed and that Allied ground forces would pull back to avoid being hit. He immediately called down an artillery strike on these crossroads, which he guessed was a likely Allied assembly point. Unfortunately for the Fusiliers Mont-Royal, the officer was right – this was the very location to which the battalion had just withdrawn. *(Author)*

Stand B2: The Frontal Assaults on May

DIRECTIONS: Return to the D562, turn left and drive south for 2.1 km to the southern edge of St-Martin-de-Fontenay. Go straight on through the mini-roundabout and immediately park where safe. Cross to the east side of the road, and stand at the 'Traversée de St-André' 13-tonne weight limit sign beside a tree.

ORIENTATION: Stand facing south looking down the D562 toward May. To the left (east) are open fields rising towards the top of the Verrières Ridge. On the right is a field then some trees; beyond – hidden from view – is the River Orne. To the front-right can be seen the triple silo structure on the northern shoulder of the ravine that runs east-southeast from the river up to May.

THE ACTION: At 2355 hours on 7 August – after the bombing had ended – the weakened Fusiliers Mont-Royal attacked south from the St-André crossroads down the road towards May supported only by the fire of some 4.2-inch mortars. Already reduced to just 40 riflemen, B Company advanced on an axis right (west) of the road while simultaneously C Company moved south to the east of the road. Behind this spearhead, A and D Companies followed on 500 metres to the rear. At 0015 hours, as C Company advanced across the fields 200 metres north-northeast of this stand, it was hit by accurate artillery fire that killed or wounded several officers and NCOs. The company nevertheless managed to close to within 350 metres of the village but the intense machine-gun fire it met caused its soldiers to become increasingly dispersed in the fields 250 metres south-east of this stand. Soon so few soldiers remained as a coherent tactical group that the company commander halted the attack and requested via radio that the battalion provide him with additional support.

Consequently, at 0150 hours, Lt-Col Gauvreau called down pre-arranged artillery concentrations on the village to restore forward momentum to the attack. When this fire subsided, B and C Companies resumed their advance, but again only made slow headway in the face of accurate defensive fire. Nevertheless, by 0230 hours a 20-strong group from B Company – by then this unit had been reduced to just 35 uninjured riflemen – had managed to fight itself forward to the northern fringes of May. As these events unfolded, the soldiers of A Company lay prone in the tall crops 200 metres north of the village (400 metres south-southwest of this stand) as German fire raked the area, waiting in vain for a successful B Company to signal them forward into the village.

By about 0250 hours Gauvreau knew that his attack had stalled irrevocably. He now withdrew his forces and reorganised them to execute a new plan of attack. As described in Stand B3, while A and B Companies resumed the battalion's previous frontal assault on May at 0315 hours to fix the Germans' attention, C and D Companies infiltrated around the right (western) flank into the village via the quarry-ravine. However, at about 0430 hours, when Gauvreau heard that this attempted infiltration had failed, he disengaged his A and B Companies from the murderous firefight that still raged north of the village and withdrew them to positions located adjacent to this stand.

View taken from Stand B2 looking south-east toward May and the triple silo structure north of the quarry-ravine. By 0230 hours, 20 soldiers of B Company had pushed south across this field to close on the northern edge of May. *(Author)*

Despite this second failure, Gauvreau understood that his Fusiliers had to secure the road through May so that the Allies could use it to resupply their spearhead mobile columns. Consequently, he decided that the Fusiliers would have to mount a third attempt to capture the village once daylight emerged, despite the risk of enfilade fire from the Feuguerolles-Bully heights west of the Orne. That morning, as the battalion prepared to mount this third assault, Gauvreau learned that three troops of Crocodile flame-throwing tanks from 141st RAC were on their way to assist this attack. Gauvreau realised that these terrifying weapons would only make his next attack more likely to achieve success if his soldiers co-operated effectively with them; once the Crocodiles entered the dangerous milieu of the village, his infantry would have to prevent *Panzerfaust*-equipped German soldiers from knocking out the tanks. Yet the Fusiliers

A view of a Crocodile flame-throwing tank in action. The successful Fusiliers Mont-Royal assault on May-sur-Orne owed much to effective co-operation with the Crocodile tanks of 141st RAC. *(TTM 329/A2)*

had never undertaken any training in close infantry cooperation with Crocodiles! Undeterred, Gauvreau hastily organised an improvised training session for his men which took place during the middle of the day once the Crocodiles had arrived. This makeshift retraining inevitably delayed the start time of the attack until 1545 hours, by which time the second phase of Totalize had already commenced.

The substantial casualties the Fusiliers had already suffered forced Gauvreau to commit the entire battalion to this two-pronged assault on the village. At 1545 hours, the western assault force – the 60 remaining soldiers of C and D Companies plus a troop of Crocodiles – advanced south toward May on an axis 50 metres west of the road. Simultaneously, the 90 riflemen of A and B Companies plus two troops of Crocodiles advanced south along an axis 100 metres east of the road. As the western force reached the north-west outskirts of May, it advanced to the rear of the houses that bordered the main road, while half of the eastern group repeated this approach on the north-east fringes of the village. Some minutes earlier, however, the rest of the eastern group had veered south-east toward Point 67 (800 metres south-east – to the front-left – of this stand) to engage the German positions located along the western fringes of the Verrières Ridge.

Despite their lack of training, the Canadian infantry and tanks soon managed to implement an effective tactical drill during this assault. As the Crocodiles advanced behind the houses on either side of the main street, the infantry covered them with small-arms fire. Then the Crocodiles fired their main guns into the nearby dwellings to suppress any residual German fire and to make gaping holes in the walls. The tanks, with the infantry clustering behind them for protection, then approached these buildings, and launched their fearsome jets of flame through these holes to set the interiors on fire. Finally, the infantry forced open the doors of these burning buildings and, once inside, finished off any German soldiers who continued to offer resistance with grenades, rifles, and bayonets.

The combination of this effective inter-arm cooperation and the terrifying impact of the jets of flame soon brought success. Although both Allied forces initially encountered fierce resistance within the village, it became increasingly apparent that the terrified defenders were not prepared to stay at their posts and face this inferno of flame and grenade, swiftly followed by the bayonet. Consequently, the western group soon advanced to a point behind the church at the junction in the village centre, where its Crocodiles flamed every hedge, ditch, or shed that might conceal machine gunners or snipers. Next, the western group consolidated the area around this junction while the eastern task force then advanced south-west and south-east out of the village, down the main road and the route to Fontenay-le-Marmion respectively. Along the main road, the Germans withdrew at the mere sight of the Crocodiles, but along the road to Fontenay they continued to resist, forcing the tanks to flame the houses before the infantry went in; here, however, the Germans soon surrendered once the flame neared their positions. By 1800 hours the Fusiliers Mont-Royal had completed their mission and secured the whole of May and the surrounding area.

Stand B3: The Infiltration Attack at May

DIRECTIONS: Continue south on the D562 for 800 metres into May, then turn right at a mini-roundabout into a road flanked by the modern church and *mairie* (an option here is to view the monuments to Operation Spring in the *mairie* gardens). After 30 metres take the right-hand fork north-west for 100 metres, then another right-hand fork north for 90 metres. Next turn left/north-west on a narrow road, and park. Walk south-east back down this road, pass through a gap in the wall to the south-west, and continue north-west across a gravel area and scrub for 130 metres to the eastern edge (top) of a ravine.

A tourer at the location for Stand B3. Gauvreau's plan to infiltrate through this ravine was only feasible during darkness. If daylight caught the infiltrators still in the ravine (and the rest of the Fusiliers attacking the village frontally), both would be enfiladed from the Feuguerolles-Bully heights west of the Orne. *(Author)*

ORIENTATION: Face west-northwest looking down into, and along the axis of, this steep-sided quarry-ravine, with the triple silo structure situated 100 metres to the north. Some 250 metres to the north-west at the bottom end of the ravine, close to the River Orne, can be seen the quadruple silo structure. Beyond these silos and the (obscured) river, are visible the commanding wooded heights of Feuguerolles-Bully, from where German fire enfiladed the Fusiliers Mont-Royal assaults on May. To the front-right and front-left, respectively, are the ravine's wooded northern and southern shoulders, while to the rear are the western outskirts of May.

THE ACTION: As outlined at Stand B2, from 0250 hours on 8 August, the Fusiliers reorganised in readiness for their second assault on May. Then, at 0315 hours, A and B Companies fixed German attention by renewing the battalion's frontal attack on May. Simultaneously, the 80 riflemen of C and D Companies moved quietly – without firing their weapons and with no artillery support – around the western flank of the German defences, aiming to infiltrate silently into the village via the difficult (and thus only lightly-defended) terrain of the quarry-ravine. Once in the western fringes of the village, Gauvreau hoped that his troops could fight their way into the centre of May and thus suppress the German fire being encountered by the continuing frontal attack; between them, the two forces might secure the village before dawn broke.

View taken from near Stand B3 looking north-west into the quarry-ravine near May-sur-Orne. *(Author)*

By 0335 hours the infiltrators had managed to cross undetected the slope that ran down towards the river around le Grand Moulin and then, once at the north-west end of the ravine, the force split into three groups. During the next 25 minutes, one group scrambled up the ravine, while the other two infiltrated through the ravine's wooded northern and southern shoulders toward the western fringes of May. By 0400 hours the infiltrators, having reached the top lip of the ravine (by this stand), had closed to just 200 metres short of the village's westernmost houses. Suddenly, however, a vigilant German guard spotted the Canadians and alerted an officer, whom the infiltrators observed dashing around his position rousing his sleeping men. Within seconds, the rudely awakened Germans had unleashed intense machine-gun and small-arms fire into the infiltrators, immediately causing casualties. In this difficult terrain, the Canadians had no hope of success now that surprise had been lost, and so they hurriedly withdrew to the main Fusilier positions. When Gauvreau learned that his infiltration attack had failed, he withdrew back up the road his A and B Companies, which were then still locked in a deadly firefight north of May. By about 0440 hours, therefore, the entire battalion was back in its previous positions beside Stand B2. This second attack on May had failed, and consequently – as already described in Stand B2 – it would not be until that afternoon that the third Fusilier assault finally captured the village.

Stand B4: The Start Line for the Assault on Tilly-la-Campagne

NOTE: From the Canadian battle for May, the tour now moves on to examine the British infantry assault on Tilly-la-Campagne.

DIRECTIONS: From your parking spot drive back south-east along the narrow road, then turn left/northwest for 1.2 km. Turn right at a mini-roundabout and continue east-northeast for 600 metres to a crossroads. Turn right/south onto the D562 for 2.8 km through May, then, after the road bends sharply right past Point 61, turn sharp left onto the D41 heading north-east for 2.7 km. Turn left at the crossroads in Fontenay-le-Marmion onto the D235 and drive north for 3 km to the crossroads with the D89. Turn right/east for 2 km, then (at la Guingette) continue on the D89 (by taking the right fork heading east, then 220 metres after passing over the N158, taking a second right fork sign-posted Hubert-Folie heading north-east for 500 metres). Then 5 metres before a mini-roundabout (signposted Hubert-Folie) turn right/south onto a gravel track for 150 metres and park.

ORIENTATION: Stand facing south-southeast looking along the track at the copse 300 metres away, which obscures the view of Tilly-la-Campagne, 2 km beyond. To the left is le Haut Grimaud industrial park, while to the right the fields of la Chasse extend across to the south-southeast course of the N158.

THE ACTION: On this spot at 2350 hours 7 August, Lt-Col Andrews' 2nd Seaforths crossed their start line and marched south-southeast along this track toward the nearby copse. The battalion's mission was to capture the German positions at Tilly-la-Campagne, which the advancing British columns had outflanked. The battalion was to attack along the 1.2-km wide sector between the axes of advances developed by the columns. Simonds hoped that 2nd Seaforths would capture Tilly before dawn so that reinforcements and supplies could be moved down to the locations secured by the columns. 2nd Seaforths had under command a 17-pounder anti-tank gun troop plus a machine-gun platoon from 1st/7th Middlesex. According to Allied intelligence, elements of three companies from the 3rd Battalion of *Oberstleutnant* (Lt-Col) Rossmann's 1055th Grenadier Regiment, part of 89th Division, defended the area in and around Tilly. The 70 men of 5th Company defended the village itself, while elements of 6th and 7th Companies had dug-in across the fields of les Noires Terres to the east, and le Val to the west.

The battalion's plan envisaged a three-pronged assault with D Company attacking the village frontally along the railway embankment, while A and B Companies respectively mounted left- and right-flanking assaults. At 2350 hours, D Company crossed the start line here at this stand, followed shortly by A and B Companies, while C Company remained in reserve. Then, at 0003 hours on 8 August, Allied artillery began to lay down a rolling barrage along a line that ran east-northeast through the level crossing west of Tilly and the orchard north of the village. Over the next 25 minutes, as the barrage rolled south-southeast at 100 metres per minute through and beyond the village, the three echeloned companies silently marched south-east down this track for 1.1 km without fire support. They then followed the track as it turned east for 100 metres until it reached the southward route of the railway embankment. Here, at about 0025 hours, D Company advanced south along the embankment, but after progressing 200 metres it met heavy machine-gun fire and accurate artillery strikes. A and B Companies also reached the turning onto the railway line at 0035 hours, and then moved south-east and south-west across the fields to mount their flanking assaults. At 0040 hours, these three companies – as described in Stand B5 – began their assault on Tilly.

If 2nd Seaforths had been able to see through the darkness, this is what they would have seen around midnight when they reached the track junction south of the copse by Point 57. Tilly church was then 1.7 km away. The infantry marched silently south-east (off the left side of the picture) before turning right onto the iron-ore railway embankment. This can be seen running left to right past the rear of the telegraph pole up to the buildings to the right of the church. (Author)

Stand B5: The Attack on Tilly

DIRECTIONS: Continue south-east on the grass track for 350 metres past a copse and take the left fork by Point 57, still a grass track, heading south-southeast for 750 metres then east for 100 metres (Tilly church soon becomes visible to the south-east). Turn right/south for 550 metres (this grass track is a disused iron-ore railway line). Park when the church is about 350 metres away.

ORIENTATION: Stand looking at Tilly's church spire. On the right (south-west) the exposed fields of le Val stretch back to the N158, while on the left are visible the orchard north of Tilly, and beyond it the road running north-east to Bourguébus.

The author's car parked at Stand B5. The church is some 350 metres away, while the orchard north of the village is just visible on the left. Around 0045 hours, A Company pushed across the fields of le Clos Neuf toward the orchard. However, intense German fire soon pinned its soldiers down. *(Author)*

THE ACTION: By 0040 hours on 8 August, D Company, 2nd Seaforths, had sought shelter on the western side of the embankment near this stand, while A and B Companies had deployed in the fields on either side; all three were now ready to assault Tilly. Next, when A Company attacked south-southeast toward the orchard north of Tilly (150 metres to the front-left of this stand), it was soon pinned down by a hail of fire. Meanwhile, to the west of the embankment, B Company pushed south-southeast toward the positions held by D Company to attack the village from the south-west. Having successfully advanced toward the level crossing (250 metres south of this stand) by 0120 hours, however, B Company's attack then petered out in the face of fierce German fire, with its now dispersed soldiers remaining pinned down in the fields of le Val. With his attack stalled, Andrews ordered his reserve unit, C Company, to move forward and restore momentum to the A Company attack on the orchard. By 0150 hours, however, C Company had also reported that accurate defensive fire had halted its advance in positions adjacent to those of A Company.

At 0200 hours, Andrews told Brigadier Cassels via the artillery net – his own radio link was down – that his stalled battalion needed further reinforcement. At 0215 hours, Cassels ordered Captain Grant Murray's D Company, 5th Seaforths, to reinforce the faltering attack on Tilly by advancing up to the railway embankment. Given that his own A and C Companies remained pinned down north of the orchard, Andrews ordered Murray to advance to the positions held by B Company west of the village. Then, at 0300 hours, Cassels debated with the 5th Seaforths' commander, Lt-Col J. Walford, whether to commit the rest of that battalion to reinvigorate Andrews' stalled attack. Walford argued that the situation was now too confused and Andrews' forces too dispersed to organise a new attack before dawn, and that anyway a two-battalion night attack across such a narrow frontage was unjustifiably risky. Cassels concurred, and so while Andrews – with the help of Murray's company – again tried to capture Tilly at 0400 hours, 152nd Brigade began to organise the massive artillery strike that would accompany this planned two-battalion daylight attack on Tilly.

View looking south along the axis of the old iron-ore railway line toward the level crossing at Point 73, just west of Tilly. By 0130 hours, B Company had passed through D Company and had advanced south along the railway toward the level crossing, aiming to attack the village from the south-west. Fierce German resistance, however, drove B Company off-course toward the south-west and then pinned its men down in the exposed fields of le Val. *(Author)*

Meanwhile, Murray's company moved up along the western axis from 0400 hours, intending to insert itself between Andrews' B and D Companies, and attack the village from the west while the 2nd Seaforths units provided fire support. When Murray's force reached its intended start line around 0440 hours, however, it found B Company badly dispersed and out of position. Consequently, only one of Murray's platoons could attack the village, while the other two provided the fire support that the 2nd Seaforths companies had been expected to supply. Unfortunately, fierce fire halted this attack, launched at 0500 hours, after inflicting 50 per cent casualties. By this time, the intense firefights that continued to rage around Tilly had also reduced the three pinned-down 2nd Seaforths' companies to just 50 effective troops each. Clearly, the assault on Tilly had now stalled irrevocably.

View of the south-west fringes of Tilly taken from near the positions held by D Company, 5th Seaforths, in the exposed fields of le Val, some 400 metres south-west of Stand B5. At 0500 hours the 40 riflemen of Sergeant Barnes' 17 Platoon attacked toward this intermittent hedge line, which ran alongside the railway. Within minutes, however, withering German fire had killed or wounded half the platoon and forced the survivors to withdraw. *(Author)*

Cassels, therefore, now ordered Walford to mount the proposed two-battalion attack at 0610 hours just after dawn had broken. Unfortunately, a pre-dawn mist then descended which prevented Walford's troops from conducting the reconnaissance required to mount the attack. Consequently, Walford postponed the attack until 1000 hours and in the interim his remaining three

5th Seaforths companies advanced toward the level crossing west of the village in the face of fierce fire. Around 0730 hours, however, as the preparations for the attack continued, Cassels learned that a squadron from 148th RAC had become available after the capture of Garcelles-Sequeville. Cassels now requested that the Shermans advance 1.9 km north-northwest toward Tilly to mount a surprise blow against the defenders' vulnerable rear.

Soldiers from the German 89th Infantry Division march into captivity near Tilly on 8 August 1944. At 1015 hours, the senior German officer still alive in Tilly – *Leutnant* Katthge – asked for a ceasefire while he assembled his remaining soldiers to surrender. Lt-Col Walford told Katthge that there would be a 35-minute truce, after which his battalions would mount their planned attack. At 1050 hours precisely, the exhausted 30-man garrison surrendered. *(NAC PA-131369)*

At 0830 hours, the Shermans rumbled, guns blazing, into the south-east fringes of the village, having caught the Germans by surprise as mist had masked their approach. For the next hour the tanks prowled around the village systematically hunting down the increasingly demoralised defenders with HE rounds and machine-gun fire. At 0950 hours, 10 minutes before the attack was to commence, Cassels heard over the brigade net that the Germans had offered to parley about their capitulation. These negotiations reached fruition at 1050 hours when a young

German lieutenant appeared from the ruins with what remained of the garrison – just 30 men. By 1100 hours, the British infantry had mopped up the remaining Germans in the fields around Tilly, taking a further 19 prisoners in the process. After an unexpectedly bitter battle, Tilly-la-Campagne was secured.

The Allied command, however, had not expected the second-rate German garrison in Tilly to offer much resistance once the advance of the British columns had isolated the village. Yet 130 supposedly mediocre German soldiers had fought off up to four British companies for 11 hours; indeed, it was only the surprise tank assault on their rear that shattered what remained of their resolve. Given this, it is not surprising that the price of liberation for the village was painfully high; like May-sur-Orne, in freeing the place from German occupation, the Allies all but destroyed it.

ENDING THE TOUR: Continue south on the grass track for 250 metres. Turn left at the level crossing and drive 150 metres past the church. Turn left/north-east, continue 1.5 km into Bourguébus and once again turn left by the church this time onto the D89. Go on for 650 metres, turn left at the mini-roundabout by Point 42 to stay on the D89 (signposted Hubert-Folie), and continue west for 2.3 km to la Guingette and the N158 to Caen.

TOUR C

'TOTALIZE' – ABORTIVE EXPLOITATION

OBJECTIVE: This tour explores the second phase of Totalize, begun around noon on 8 August, when Allied armour attempted to advance rapidly south to the high ground north of Falaise.

DURATION/SUITABILITY: This tour will take most of a day by car. It is too long to be completed as a walking tour and is not particularly suitable for cyclists because of the proportion of the route on dual carriageway. It is suitable for those with mobility difficulties, although such tourers may find the off-road sections, particularly along the Chemin Haussé, uncomfortable. Again, the tour map will help plan alternative routes that use tarmac roads. Stand C4 involves a strenuous 10-minute climb and should only be attempted by tourers who feel comfortable with such an undertaking, and who have appropriate footwear.

Stand C1: Wittmann's Last Battle

DIRECTIONS: Drive south from Caen on the N158 to la Jalousie intersection and join the D23 south-west for 300 metres. Turn left/east onto the D23a for 400 metres (passing over the N158) then north-west for 250 metres. Take the right-hand fork north-northwest for 100 metres, then turn sharp right onto the road parallel to the N158 (signposted Cintheaux). Continue south for 600 metres, then turn left into a lane heading east-northeast for 500 metres. Park where this lane bends left.

View taken from Stand C1 looking south-west towards the buildings beside the N158. Wittmann's tank was knocked out 40 metres to the left of the red-roofed, creamed-walled building. Note the line that runs from the camera toward this building marked by the yellowish colour variation discernable in the crops – this used to be a track but was cleared in the 1990s. Wittmann's Tigers were close to this track when Allied fire struck them, with one of them being destroyed at the spot where this stand is located. *(Author)*

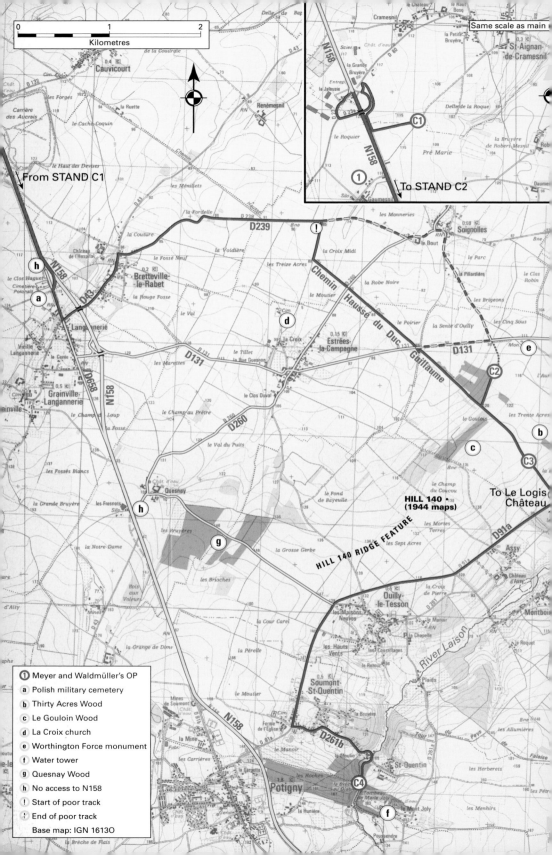

Kilometres

0   1   2

Same scale as main

From STAND C1

To STAND C2

To Le Logis Château

HILL 140 •
(1944 maps)

HILL 140 RIDGE FEATURE

Base map: IGN 1613O

① Meyer and Waldmüller's OP

a Polish military cemetery

b Thirty Acres Wood

c Le Gouloin Wood

d La Croix church

e Worthington Force monument

f Water tower

g Quesnay Wood

h No access to N158

! Start of poor track

¡ End of poor track

ORIENTATION: Face south-southwest toward the red-roofed building next to the N158, 700 metres distant; 40 metres east of this building Allied fire brewed up Wittmann's Tiger tank, killing him. Visible to the front-left are the open fields that stretch south to les Jardinets, to the front-right and right the N158 running north to la Jalousie and beyond, and to the right rear the water tower by the D80 road south of Cramesnil. Situated 300 metres away to the left-rear is a 250 metres-long tree-hedge that runs roughly west–east through Delle de la Roque; it may have been from behind this hedge that a Sherman Firefly tank fired the shot that ended Wittmann's career.

Warrant Officer Adolf Bochniak, Sergeant Stanislaw Stochel, and 2nd Lieutenant Mical Prusak from the 1st Polish Armoured Division sit on the turret of a destroyed Panther from Battlegroup *Waldmüller*. At 1220 hours a force of 20 tanks and 200 panzergrenadiers from this command struck north-west toward St-Aignan from the les Jardinets area, 600 metres south-east of Wittmann's Tigers. This Panther is probably one of the six tanks from this force that succumbed to Allied fire during the operation. *(NAC PA-115490)*

THE ACTION: The circumstances behind the bold riposte mounted by Wittmann's four Tigers from 1220 hours on 8 August have been described in the history section. At that time, Wittmann's troop moved off from concealed positions behind a hedge near les Jardinets, 900 metres south-southeast of this stand. The tanks rumbled north-northwest one behind the other on an axis parallel to, but 100 metres east of, the Caen–Falaise road. As they advanced, the Tigers periodically stopped in shallow gullies to fire at long range to the north-west at some Sherbrooke Fusiliers' tanks west of the main road opposite Hill 122. At a range of 1.8 km, the Tigers knocked out several Shermans, whereas at this distance not even the regiment's few 17-pounder Fireflies stood much chance of damaging the Tigers. Meanwhile, nearby elements of Battlegroup *Waldmüller* also thrust north-northwest; between them, the two German forces were to secure the high ground south of the St-Aignan, and thus disrupt the imminent Allied armoured thrust south.

Wittmann seemed to anticipate fire from the main road to the north-northwest, for he deployed his four tanks in line ahead to minimise the target they presented to this direction. In so doing, however, he rendered his tanks vulnerable to fire from the north-east – from the orchards south of St-Aignan; Wittmann's available intelligence had probably not revealed that A Squadron, 1st Northants Yeomanry, had pushed forward from St-Aignan to secure these orchards just 90 minutes previously. Around 1235 hours, the squadron's No. 3 Troop sighted the Tigers advancing north, 1.2 km away. Sergeant Gordon's Sherman Firefly – the only tank in the troop capable of stopping Wittmann at this range – moved forward to the southern edge of the orchard to get a better field of fire. At 1240 hours, when the Tigers had closed to 900 metres – having neared the red-roofed building – Gordon's Firefly opened fire, while simultaneously Sherbrooke Fusiliers and 144th RAC Fireflies engaged Wittmann's tanks at a range of 1.3 km from west of the main road and Hill 122, respectively.

According to the 1st Northants Yeomanry war diary, Sergeant Gordon's gunner – Trooper Joe Ekins – fired two shots at the rear Tiger, which brewed up. Next, the second Tiger turned right toward the north-east and fired three shots at Gordon's Firefly as it reversed into the cover of the orchard, during which process Gordon was wounded. The leader of No. 3 Troop, Lieutenant James, took command of the Firefly and moved to a new firing position. Then, at 1247 hours Ekins apparently fired one shot at the second tank, which exploded in a ball of flame. Some of A Squadron's standard Shermans then advanced south out of the woods to engage the Tigers at such close range that they stood some chance of damaging them, but this inadvertently hampered

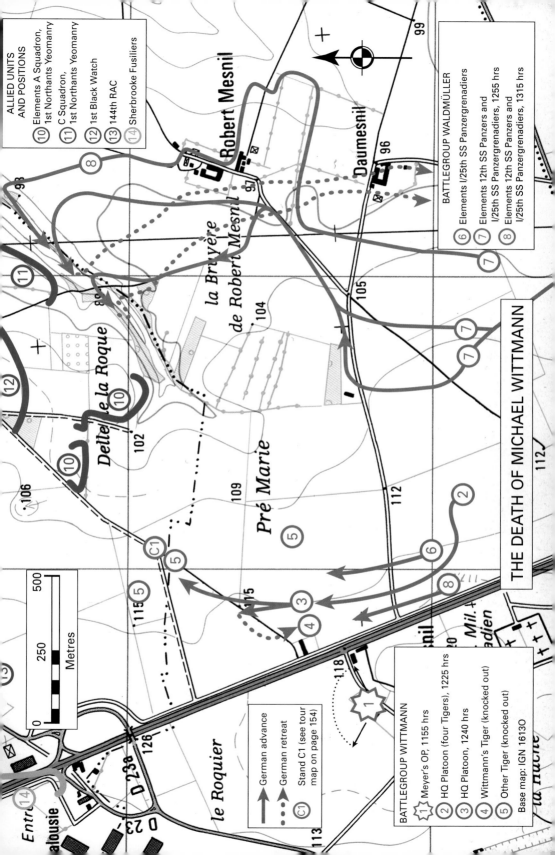

THE DEATH OF MICHAEL WITTMANN

ALLIED UNITS AND POSITIONS

- ⑩ Elements A Squadron, 1st Northants Yeomanry
- ⑪ C Squadron, 1st Northants Yeomanry
- ⑫ 1st Black Watch
- ⑬ 144th RAC
- ⑭ Sherbrooke Fusiliers

BATTLEGROUP WALDMÜLLER

- ⑥ Elements I/25th SS Panzergrenadiers
- ⑦ Elements 12th SS Panzers and I/25th SS Panzergrenadiers, 1255 hrs
- ⑧ Elements 12th SS Panzers and I/25th SS Panzergrenadiers, 1315 hrs

BATTLEGROUP WITTMANN

- ① Meyer's OP, 1155 hrs
- ② HQ Platoon (four Tigers), 1225 hrs
- ③ HQ Platoon, 1240 hrs
- ④ Wittmann's Tiger (knocked out)
- ⑤ Other Tiger (knocked out)

Base map: IGN 16130

→ German advance

⤏ German retreat

C1 Stand C1 (see tour map on page 154)

Metres

0   250   500

Robert Mesnil

Daumesnil

la Bruyère de Robert Mesnil

Delle de la Roque

Pré Marie

le Roquier

Entre... alousie

D 238   126   D 23

Mil. + ...dien

the fire delivered by Ekins' Firefly. The ensuing hail of Sherman fire fell upon the lead German tank – Wittmann's command Tiger. While these rounds failed to penetrate the tank's thick armour, they nevertheless so damaged the vehicle that it veered off erratically, seemingly out of control. By 1252 hours, Wittmann's crippled tank had come to a halt 40 metres east of the building adjacent to the main road, and now Ekins' Firefly fired two shots that apparently caused the stricken Tiger to burst into flame; from this inferno none of the crew escaped. Of course, at this moment, longer-range Firefly fire from the Sherbrooke Fusiliers and 144th RAC was also raining down on this area, so it is impossible to be certain that it was Ekins' rounds that finished off the legendary German commander. But if Wittmann died in this encounter what happened to his body? This question remained unanswered until 1983, when his remains were found in a communal grave located near to the red-roofed building. This discovery finally proved that Wittmann, as befitted his legendary reputation, had met a warrior's death attempting to stem the Totalize offensive.

View from Stand C1 looking north-east to the tree-hedge at Delle de la Roque, behind which in 1944 there was an orchard. It was from behind this western part of the tree-line that No. 3 Troop, A Squadron, 1st Northants Yeomanry, engaged Wittmann's tanks. It is claimed that gunner Joe Ekins' Sherman Firefly was the vehicle that ultimately destroyed Wittmann's Tiger. *(Author)*

Stand C2: The Worthington Force Position

DIRECTIONS: Retrace your route to la Jalousie intersection and join the N158 south for 5.7 km. At the Langannerie intersection turn left by Point 115 onto the D658 (the original Caen–Falaise road which deviates from the N158 here). Head south for 450 metres and turn left at the mini-roundabout onto the D43 (signposted Bretteville-le-Rabet). Drive back over the N158 into Bretteville and turn right at the crossroads onto the D239 (signposted Soignolles). Continue east for 1.5 km to Point 91 (here the Chemin Haussé du Duc Guillaume, a grass track, joins from the left). Stay on the D239 east for 750 metres more until Point 85. Turn right onto a gravel track south-southwest for 500 metres to Point 88 and then left onto the Chemin Haussé (along which Worthington Force travelled) heading south-east cautiously for 1.4 km to the junction with the D131 (you can make an optional detour here 1 km east to the Worthington Force Monument). Continue south-east on the Chemin Haussé for 900 metres then turn left at Point 120 onto a grass track heading north-northeast (along the edge of a wood) for 500 metres until you are near Point 111. Park after the grass track bends right and then sharply left.

View taken from the north-west fringes of the Worthington Force position looking north-west across open country. The raised Chemin Haussé – along which Worthington Force advanced – can be seen running south-east from the right background toward the wood in the left foreground (which is close to Point 111). On the left, above the trees, is Estrées-la-Campagne. *(Author)*

BATTLEFIELD TOURS

ALTERNATIVE ROUTE: Instead of turning right at Point 85, continue on the D239 for 1.1 km. Turn left at le Bout and follow the D260 for 300 metres into Soignolles; take the right fork (east) for 150 metres then turn right (by a Calvary at Point 72) heading south for 300 metres. This time take the left-hand fork south-east for 1.1 km and park by the intersection with the D131 at Point 98. Walk south down the grass track for 450 metres to Stand C2.

ORIENTATION: Stand facing south-southeast looking across the fields of les Trente Acres, past the small copse 250 metres away by Point 122, to the wood 900 metres away, here termed 'Thirty Acres Wood'. To the front-left and front-right are the fields covering la Plate Delle and the summit of Hill 140. La Croix church is visible 2.5 km away to the rear-right, as is la Pillardière, 900 metres to the rear-left, and the twin flag poles (perhaps with Canadian flag flying) at the Worthington Force Monument (450 metres north-east by the D131 road).

View from Stand C2 looking south-east across the Worthington Force position. On the right is the copse and in the background is 'Thirty Acres Wood'. *(Author)*

THE ACTION: The advance of Worthington Force to les Trente Acres by 0640 hours on 9 August has been recounted in the main narrative. The force that dug in at this location comprised the 55 tanks of B, C, and HQ Squadrons, British Columbia Regiment, one whole and one part Algonquin Regiment company, plus supporting arms. The rest of Worthington Force had become separated in the night and these units never got to this position.

Unfortunately, by then, *SS-Obersturmführer* (Lt) Bernhard-Georg Meitzel, a *Hitlerjugend* staff officer, had spotted the Canadian force from the south-west slopes of Hill 140, 1.9 km south-west of this stand. Meitzel's vehicle evaded the fire directed at it and raced back to the 12th SS Panzer Regiment concentration area in Quesnay wood, where he reported to Max Wünsche.

Even worse, around 0615 hours members of the *Hitlerjugend* divisional staff – including Meyer himself – had witnessed Meitzel's escape from the observation posts at la Brèche au Diable and the Tombeau de Marie Joly, 4.7 km south-southwest of Point 122. Meyer then hurried to Quesnay wood where he personally supervised the launching of an immediate attack by Battlegroup *Waldmüller*. Around 0740 hours, a dozen of Worthington's Shermans advanced to 'Thirty Acres Wood', from where they could observe German movement toward the Hill 140 feature. It seemed a timely move, for just minutes after the Shermans had reached the wood their crews spotted the first Panther tanks approaching from the south-west. Yet, at this moment, few of Worthington's soldiers could have possibly foreseen the bloody catastrophe about to engulf them.

Stand C3: The Destruction of Worthington Force

DIRECTIONS: Retrace your route from the Stand C2 parking spot to Point 120 (if you reached C2 by the alternative route drive west on the D131 and then south-west on the Chemin Haussé to Point 120). Turn left onto the Chemin Haussé du Duc Guillaume, head south-east for 1 km, and stop opposite 'Thirty Acres Wood'.

ORIENTATION: Face south-west with 'Thirty Acres Wood' to the rear looking toward the summit of Hill 140. Some 900 metres distant to the south-east is le Logis Château (in the wooded Laison Valley south-east of the Chemin Haussé), while Stand C2 (the Worthington Force position) is 1.1 km to the north-west.

THE ACTION: Around 0720 hours, two SS battlegroups set off from Quesnay wood – 3.8 km west-southwest of this stand, beyond the summit of Hill 140 – to destroy the Canadian force dug in around les Trente Acres. The first group of 18 panzers and some panzergrenadiers headed toward the summit of Hill 140 (directly toward this stand), from where they engaged the Canadian forces. The second group, of eight Tigers plus panzergrenadiers, moved south-west along the road to les Maisons Neuves and thence east-northeast along the road that skirted the southern slopes of the Hill 140 feature (now the D91a) until it reached le Logis Château. Here, the force swung north and north-west through the open fields to strike the Canadian position from the south-east and east. Around 0800 hours, the leading panzers from both groups engaged the Shermans deployed in 'Thirty Acres Wood', and within 20 minutes had knocked out all 12 of them.

View from Stand C3 looking south-east across the southern slopes of Hill 140 to le Logis Château; the River Laison runs through the woods visible beyond the château. The second group from Battlegroup *Waldmüller* attacked Worthington Force from this direction. *(Author)*

Subsequently, Worthington Force informed 4th Brigade that it was under attack and requested that artillery fire be brought down on the Germans who were now just 450 metres south and south-east of its position (450 metres north and north-east of this stand). Sadly, because both Worthington Force and the higher Allied command still believed that the force was on Hill 195, this artillery fire landed accurately on a spot some 7 km away. Even worse, by then the attacking SS forces had surrounded the Canadian task force. Encircled and lacking indirect fire support, the dire situation the battlegroup faced deteriorated after 0907 hours when its communication links fell silent, presumably after succumbing to German fire. After this loss of contact, 4th Brigade ordered the Governor General's Foot Guards to ready themselves to rescue Worthington Force by advancing to the latter's perceived location on Hill 195.

Intense fire continued to rake the position throughout that morning, inflicting heavy casualties on Worthington's command. Realising that his wounded could not be treated in such conditions, the colonel ordered his few still-operational half-tracks to carry them to safety by breaking out toward the north-west. Miraculously, the column successfully escaped through the gauntlet of German fire back to the Allied lines. Yet in the confusion that beset this ordeal by fire the escapees failed to ascertain – as Worthington hoped they would – the task force's precise location. Consequently, the missing battlegroup remained lost both to itself and to the Allied command. Subsequently, the inferno of fire that engulfed the Canadian position reached a new crescendo when Allied fighter-bombers inadvertently attacked them, understandably not expecting to find friendly forces in this location. After Worthington's mortar crews warned off the Typhoons with yellow identification smoke, the aircraft repeatedly returned to strafe the nearby German positions – support that earned them hearty cheers from the beleaguered troops below. Unfortunately, this succour did not alter the fate awaiting the battlegroup because news of where this friendly force was located somehow failed to reach II Corps.

Waldmüller's forces continued their attacks until, by early afternoon, just eight of the 55 Canadian tanks that had reached les Trente Acres remained operational. Worthington now ordered these vehicles to mount a break-out attempt. Somehow the tanks managed to evade the German fire as they raced north to reach the safety of the nearby Polish positions. The information then garnered concerning the location of Worthington Force subsequently led the Canadian Grenadier Guards and the Poles to mount separate bids to rescue the beleaguered battlegroup. Sadly, intense German fire delivered from Quesnay wood and Hill 140 halted both these efforts during the course of the afternoon and early evening. Meanwhile, around 1830 hours the Germans had mounted another determined assault on the remnants of Worthington Force. Every Canadian soldier still capable of firing a weapon, including the wounded and the tank crews whose vehicles had been wrecked, fought back desperately with small

THE DESTRUCTION OF WORTHINGTON FORCE

ALLIED UNITS AND POSITIONS

1. Worthington Force, 0400 hrs
2. Worthington Force position, 0640 hrs
3. Three troops, British Columbia Regiment, 0740 hrs
4. Remnants of three troops, British Columbia Regiment, 0820 hrs
5. Wounded, platoon strength, *c.* 1030 hrs
6. Two troops, British Columbia Regiment, *c.* 1400 hrs
7. Two depleted infantry sections, 2030 hrs
8. Canadian Grenadier Guards
9. 1st Polish Armoured Division

Soignolles

Chemin Haussé

Estrées-la-Campagne

le Val

C2

C3 Thirty Acres Wood

111

111

132

le Tesson

→ Allied advance

••••► Allied retreat

C2 Stand (see tour map on page 154)

Base map: IGN 1613O

GERMAN UNITS

10. Company, I/25th SS Panzergrenadiers and company, 12th SS Panzers, 0730 hrs
11. Company, I/25th SS Panzergrenadiers and two platoons, 101st Heavy SS Panzer Battalion, 0800 hrs
12. 1st Company, 12th SS Anti-Tank Battalion
13. Battlegroup 85th Infantry Division
14. 12th SS Escort Company

0   0.5   1

Kilometres

arms and grenades, and managed to drive off this latest strike. Sadly, as Worthington strove to orchestrate this resistance an incoming mortar round fatally injured him. Subsequently, as the battlegroup's fortunes plummeted further, hope appeared in the distance as Polish tanks, advancing south-east from Estrées, again neared its position. This glimmer of salvation soon dwindled, however, as a storm of German tank and artillery fire halted the Polish advance 1.1 km short of le Gouloin woods.

The final curtain now came down on the tragedy of Worthington Force's first and last action. Around 2030 hours, as dusk descended, a succession of German assaults finally overran the Canadian position. In this final encounter, only two groups of seven Canadian soldiers, each led by a lieutenant, managed to fight their way out through the encircling forces to reach the nearby Polish positions. Despite the heroic resistance it offered that day, Worthington Force had been decimated. At various times during the day small groups managed to escape back to Allied lines, but these amounted to around just 120 personnel. The fact that a bizarre combination of Allied errors, misunderstandings, and bad luck had contributed to the brutal demise of Worthington Force only compounded the sense of loss Simonds' felt at the cutting short of so many Canadian servicemen's lives. Shining out to offset this, however, was the astonishing courage displayed by Worthington's troops in the face of appalling adversity.

The Worthington Force Monument commemorates 'courage and sacrifice' that remain 'unsurpassed in the annals of the Canadian Army'. Understandably, given this valour, the monument remains silent about the force becoming so lost that it ended up more than 6 km away from its intended objective. *(Author)*

Stand C4: La Brèche au Diable

DIRECTIONS: Continue south-east on the Chemin Haussé heading downhill for 700 metres then turn right (south-west) onto the D91a for 3 km. Turn left onto the D261b (at a mini-roundabout in southern Soumont-St-Quentin) and continue east-

Panoramic view from la Brèche looking 4.7 km north-east toward the summit of Hill 140, with 'Thirty Acres Wood' visible on the right horizon. *(Author)*

southeast for 1.1 km past le Moulin. Turn right beyond Point 105 onto a gravel track and continue south through a wood for 250 metres. Park by the River Laison and use the information board to orientate yourself for the steep 10-minute climb (appropriate footwear is recommended) up through trees to Stand C4 at la Brèche au Diable, the small clearing on the western edge of the deep rock gorge. (An option here is also to climb from the parking spot up to the OP at Tombeau de Marie Joly, but note that trees now obscure the view obtainable from here in 1944).

ORIENTATION: Stand in this small clearing looking north-northeast toward Hill 140, 3.5 km distant on the horizon.

THE ACTION: The surrounding woods obscure the view obtainable from la Brèche au Diable except in a north-easterly direction toward Hill 140, where 'Thirty Acres Wood' is visible. It was here at 0615 hours that a piece of appalling ill fortune befell Worthington Force. As *Hitlerjugend* staff officers scanned the horizon from la Brèche they saw, in the dim half-light of pre-dawn, the dust thrown up by Worthington's vehicles as they moved along the Chemin Haussé toward les Trente Acres. Simultaneously, Kurt Meyer witnessed this same event from the Tombeau de Marie Joly OP, situated 150 metres away across the

gorge. This chance detection of the Canadian battlegroup triggered the chain of events that led to the subsequent destruction of Worthington Force.

La Brèche au Diable, the vantage point on the western edge of the rocky Laison gorge. The nearby woods obscure much of the view but 'Thirty Acres Wood' can be seen on the left-horizon. *(Author)*

ENDING THE TOUR: Retrace your route along the D261b and D91a for 3 km to les Maisons Neuves and turn left toward Quesnay for 300 metres (to the north-east is the terrain across which the Germans advanced to strike Worthington Force). Go on north-west for 1.8 km (through Quesnay wood). Turn right by the church onto the D260 for 250 metres (here, as the D260 bends right, is a view of the N158 to the left/north-west showing how the wood dominated the main road); continue on the D260 for 1.9 km. Take the left fork (south-west of Estrées) heading north for 100 metres, then turn left at the crossroads onto the D131 for 2 km towards Langannerie, to join the N158 to Caen.

TOUR D

'TRACTABLE'

OBJECTIVE: This tour explores the Allied break-in across the River Laison and the subsequent exploitation toward Falaise.

DURATION/SUITABILITY: This tour will take about half a day by car. It may be suitable for cyclists (taking a full day) but is too long to be completed as a walking tour. It is suitable for those with mobility difficulties, but such tourers may find the small amount of off-road travel just before Stand D4 uncomfortable.

Stand D1: The Tractable Start Line

DIRECTIONS: Drive south from Caen on the N158 to Langannerie and turn left onto the D658 by Point 115. Continue south-east for 900 metres, then turn left/east onto the D131 (pass over the N158) for 2.3 km to Estrées-la-Campagne (note la Croix church 700 metres left). Go straight on at the crossroads for 20 metres, the turn left onto the D260 (signposted Soignolles). Continue north-east for 2.3 km (go straight on at le Bout crossroads) into Soignolles. Take the right fork, heading east for 150 metres, then turn right/south (by a Calvary at Point 72), for 300 metres. Take the left fork and go on 600 metres (through la Pillardière). Park beyond the edge of a tree-hedge on the left.

ORIENTATION: Face south-southeast looking down the road at the fields of la Sente d'Ouilly and les Cinq Sous, and beyond to the woods around Point 122 (near which the Worthington Force position was located). To the south-east are visible the flag poles at the Worthington Force Monument, while 2.1 km to the south-west is la Croix church and nearby Estrées-la-Campagne.

View from Stand C2 looking north-west across les Brigeons to la Pillardière; Stand D1 is just in front of the right-hand house. Around 1205 hours, having crossed the 'Tractable' start line, Governor General's Foot Guards Shermans rumbled south-southeast from the trees to the right of this stand on an axis to the right of the furthest haystack. Within minutes the tanks had plunged into the smoke screen that hundreds of Allied guns had begun to generate. *(Author)*

THE ACTION: From this stand is visible the terrain over which the initial attacks of Tractable unfolded. The 1.3-km wide start line for the 3rd Division (western) grouping ran from Estrées – 1.8 km to the west of this stand – to la Robe Noire (850 metres north-west of this stand). Some 1 km north-east of the latter area, the 1-km wide start line for the eastern (4th Division) grouping ran north-east from Soignolles to near Point 85 (to the right-rear of this stand). Between them, these two groups fielded 480 tanks, 1,500 vehicles and 12,000 men, deployed in three echelons to a depth of 3 km. This stand focuses on the actions of the eastern group, which unfolded to the east of the viewer at this location.

At 1130 hours on 14 August, the eastern grouping's first echelon – 4th Canadian Armoured Brigade plus the Lake Superior Regiment – rumbled south-southeast at 18 km/hr from its assembly area toward the start line, 1 km north-east of this

Kilometres

| 0 | 1 | 2 |

D260
la Voidière
la Croix Midi
le Bout
le Parc
les Roque
D131
le Moutier
la Robe Noire
la Pillardière
le Clos Robin
les Brigeons
D1
les Cinq Sous
① ② ③
le Val
a
le Poirier
la Sente d'Ouilly
b
Mon
D131
D131
le Tillet
la Croix
la Rue Guesnon
Estrées-la-Campagne
la Hogue
l'Aumône
c
Rouvres
les Marettes
D131
le Champ au Prêtre
le Clos Duval
D260
le Trente Acres
la Plate Delle
le Goulon
e
le Prunier
Queshay
le Val du Puits
Bne
le Champ du Coucou
la Fosse aux Loups
le Logis Chât
le Moulin de Rouvres
les Bruyères
HILL 140 (1944 maps)
les Mortes Terres
le Vieux Jardin
River Laison
la Grosse Gerbe
les Sept Acres
D91a
Assy
la Mayen
les Brioches
la Croix de Pierre
Château d'Assy
Ouilly-le-Tesson
D261
Montboint
la Cour Carel
la Perelle
les Maisons Neuves
le Manoir
D3
RN
le Sommier
de Dîme
RN
Chapelle
le Roquet
les Hauts Vents
les Courtillages
les Allumières
la Chardonneuse
N158
D91a
le Retour
Plaids
la Couturelle
les Feugres
Soumont-St-Quentin
Pays
la Bruyère
Cim
Falaise
Tour
les Herberets
Olendon
les Carrières
le Manoir
St-Quentin
les Menhirs
les Pétrelles
Potigny
la Brèche au Diable
le Mont Joly
Tombeau de Marie Joly
POINT 170 (1944 maps)
la Hunière
Poussendre
la Fossette
le Haut Clos
la Sommière
la Pierre
les Sabines
Tassilly
l'Ormeau
le Châtelet
la Grande Bruyère
HILL 184 (1944 maps)
D261a
Bois de Catillon
COMMUNE DE BONS-TASSILLY
le Haut du Bois d'Epaney
Bois de Catillon
la Pièce
les Grêles
④
les Vingt Acres
Sur le Mont
POINT 175 (1944 maps)
le Castillon
f
Bas de Catillon
N158
D658
! ! !
D4
la Ronce
D246
la Couture Morel
le Coudray
Soulangy
Maison Deschamps

① Governor General's Foot Guards
② British Columbia Regiment
③ Canadian Grenadier Guards
④ Start point, 1st Canadian Scottish and 1st Hussars' attack
a La Croix church
b Worthington Force monument
c Silos
d Bar-brasserie le Triangle
e Thirty Acres Wood
f Farm warehouse

Base maps: IGN 1613E, IGN 1613O, IGN 1614E, IGN 1614O

stand. Separated by a 600-metre gap, the six vehicle-wide Governor General's Foot Guards and Canadian Grenadier Guards columns spearheaded the brigade's western and eastern axes of advance, respectively. Behind these regiments, the British Columbia Regiment – hastily rebuilt after its 9 August debacle – and then the Lake Superior Regiment also moved forward from their assembly areas. At 1200 hours the two spearhead regiments crossed the start line, and charged south into the Allied smoke screen. Despite this protective shroud of smoke, these 240 Shermans nevertheless encountered sustained – albeit somewhat random – German anti-tank and artillery defensive fire.

As these two columns crossed the fields between le Clos Robin and Point 85 (on the D239 road), some 500–1,700 metres north-east of this stand, they began to disintegrate due to the poor visibility, with tanks veering off in all directions as their drivers became hopelessly lost. All the British Columbia and Lake Superior drivers could do to navigate, anyway, was follow the tracks made by the preceding vehicles, assuming the latter were still on course. In the ensuing chaos – exacerbated when German fire destroyed Lt-Col Scott's command tank – many of his Foot Guards tanks became inextricably mixed up with those of the Grenadier Guards column. Despite these problems, by 1220 hours this fragmenting mass of 240 tanks had nevertheless managed to reach the road – the modern D131 – that ran west from Estrées to Maizières (1.2 km to the front-left of this stand).

Behind this armour, the grouping's second echelon – 8th Infantry Brigade – then advanced south, again navigating by following the tracks left on the ground by the preceding tanks. Between 1233 and 1245 hours, the embussed Queen's Own Rifles and Régiment de la Chaudière – deployed on the eastern and western axis, respectively – crossed the start line. The former then advanced south-east behind the Grenadier Guards toward Maizières while the latter headed south-southeast behind the Foot Guards toward Rouvres. To the rear of these battalions, the North Shore Regiment advanced on foot as brigade reserve. Next, around 1420 hours, the grouping's third echelon – 10th Brigade's three lorried infantry columns, each supported by a South Alberta squadron – began to move south-east from their assembly areas south of St-Sylvain toward the start line. As these 200 lorries rumbled south, the infantrymen they carried shouted, waved their caps, and made Native American war cries to express

Sherman tanks from 4th Canadian Armoured Division advance from their assembly area up a gentle rise toward the 'Tractable' start line, between Soignolles and Point 85, 1130–1200 hours on 14 August 1944. *(NAC PA-114064)*

their high spirits! At 1510 hours, this dense vehicular mass crossed the start line and plunged into the smoke screen. The combination of smoke, flame, and dust so restricted these columns' visibility that they – like their predecessors – disintegrated as they advanced through the fields east of this stand to reach the modern D131 road around 1530 hours.

Stand D2: Crossing the Laison at Rouvres

DIRECTIONS: Continue south-east for 600 metres, then turn left onto the D131 for 450 metres past the monument. Turn right/south-east downhill (past 'Thirty Acres Wood' to the right) for 2 km to a crossroads (near some silos). Turn left/east onto the D91a (signposted Argences) toward Rouvres for 250 metres, then turn right at a mini-roundabout (signposted Olendon) by *le Triangle Bar-Brasserie*. After 250 metres turn right and park by the church. Walk back to the main road, turn right and make your way to the bridge over the Laison.

ORIENTATION: Stand on the bridge facing toward the church.

THE ACTION: Around 1255 hours on 14 August, Major Gordon's B Squadron, 1st Hussars – having failed to find a safe fording point across the Laison around Assy – headed north-east along the northern bank toward Rouvres, where according to their maps, a road bridge spanned the stream. Around 1330 hours, having continued past several risky fording spots, the squadron's 17 operational Shermans reached Rouvres and moved past the church toward the bridge. Gordon intended to cross the Laison here and then subsequently advance 6.4 km south-west toward the Hussars' objective, Hill 184. At the bridge, however, the tanks encountered engineers surveying the damaged structure who reported that it was then unusable. Undaunted, Gordon then ordered one of his tanks to attempt to ford the Laison close to the bridge, but the Sherman bogged down in the soft stream bed.

These setbacks forced Gordon to lead his tanks through the streets of Rouvres to find another safe crossing spot. As they searched, the Shermans encountered sporadic German small-arms fire but little sustained opposition. The tanks machine-gunned any houses that they suspected held German troops, and set a barn on fire with HE rounds, causing a truck inside to explode. After fruitlessly searching for an alternative crossing, Gordon concluded that he would have to risk using the damaged bridge. When the Shermans got back to the bridge at 1400 hours, they found that British engineering vehicles had already dropped fascines into the stream to fill the largest gaps in the twisted structure. The squadron's lead Sherman then inched its way across the straining bridge-cum-fascine structure while other tank crews anxiously monitored the stability of the improvised crossing. After five anxious minutes the tank safely reached the southern end of the bridge, seemingly without further weakening the fragile crossing.

Subsequently, Gordon's remaining tanks crossed the stream using this precarious structure. When all of them had made it across, they headed south-west off the road and assembled in the low ground just south of the river (50 metres to the west of this stand). Here Gordon reorganised his squadron and quickly formulated a new plan for the next stage of the attack – the seizure of the ridge south of the village that stretched south-west toward Montboint and le Sommier. By around 1500 hours, as

Then: View taken on 16 August from the Laison's flooded southern bank looking north-west at the wrecked Rouvres church and the repaired bridge. Also visible are the fascines placed in the river on 14 August and a Governor General's Foot Guards Sherman bogged down in the soft stream bed. *(NAC PA-131270)*

Now: Modern view of the repaired and remodelled Rouvres church taken from the same spot as the photograph of 16 August 1944. *(Author)*

these 16 Shermans prepared for this next mission, No. 1 and 2 Troops, 80th Assault Squadron, Royal Engineers, had completed two additional fascine crossings of the Laison 100 metres and 400 metres east of the bridge. In addition, within a few hours the engineers had sufficiently rebuilt the twisted bridge so that it could safely take 40-ton loads. Using these three structures other 1st Hussars Shermans, as well as the bulk of 4th Brigade, reached the southern bank of the Laison during the rest of that afternoon and early evening.

Stand D3: Flaming Forward at Montboint

DIRECTIONS: Retrace your route to the D91a and turn left, south-west, for 2.7 km. Turn left at Point 109 (toward le Roquet). Continue straight on for 750 metres (go straight on at the Point 93 crossroads after 350 metres) to a crossroads and park on the right. Walk back up the road for 350 metres and stop 50 metres beyond the second, northern, bridge.

ORIENTATION: Stand facing south-west, 50 metres north of the northern bridge that spans the Laison's seasonally dry northern course. Some 100 metres to the front-right an intermittent tree-hedge runs to an isolated tree. About 50 metres to the front-left, the seasonally dry northern course heads south-west, while 75 metres beyond it a tree-hedge lines the southern course. To the rear Assy Château is visible 400 metres away.

THE ACTION: At 1220 hours on 14 August, the embussed Stormont, Dundas, and Glengarry Highlanders – part of the western grouping's second echelon – crossed the start line and advanced south to the woods around Assy, where its soldiers debussed at 1255 hours. The infantry then assaulted the positions held by 6th Company of 85th Division's 1053rd Grenadier Regiment. By 1340 hours the Highlanders had cleared the area down to the northern branch of the Laison except for Assy

FLAMING FORWARD AT MONTBOINT

Chateau d'Assy

River Laison

To LE ROQUET

RN

CANADIAN UNITS AND POSITIONS

① B Company, Stormont, Dundas and Glengarry Highlanders
② Section commander's Wasp
③ Wasp
④ Second in command's Wasp

GERMAN UNITS AND POSITIONS

⑤ First machine gun
⑥ Second machine gun
⑦ Third machine gun
⑧ Fourth machine gun
⑨ 6/1053rd Grenadiers positions
⑩ Tiger tank

〰〰 German trenches

Base map: IGN 16130

Metres
0   50   100

Château, which its B Company only secured at 1420 hours after bitter fighting. Subsequently, by late afternoon, B Company had assembled east of the Point 109–le Roquet road on a 100 metres frontage located 50 metres north-east of the bridge over the Laison's dried-up northern course. As the company struck south-west to seize both this bridge, and the one 75 metres further south, however, the fire from four well-sited machine guns immediately stymied the attack. A Tiger tank some 800 metres north-west near Point 109, prevented B Company from making a right-flanking strike, while additional machine guns to the south-west prevented any left-flanking attack mounted south of the Laison's twin branches. The only alternative for B Company to achieve its mission – a frontal assault – would probably have incurred unacceptably high casualties.

View taken from the Point 93–le Roquet road about 50 metres north-west of Stand D3 (where the section commander's Wasp deployed) looking south-west toward the fields in which four German machine guns were sited. *(Author)*

Around 1700 hours, B Company cleverly resolved this tactical problem by calling forward a section of three flame-throwing fully-tracked carriers known, appropriately, as Wasps. The carriers, having headed through Assy and past the château, moved through the positions held by B Company and deployed in front of the infantry facing south-west, 80 metres short of the Point 109–le Roquet road. The section commander's Wasp deployed on the northern axis, the second-in-command's vehicle

A Wasp infantry-carrier in action. The action at Montboint on 14 August demonstrated that the combat power of the Wasp relied as much on the terrifying psychological impact exerted by its powerful flame-gun as on the weapon's devastating physical effect. After witnessing three Wasps swiftly dispatch the three machine guns manned by their comrades, the terrified crew of the 'fourth' German machine gun understandably grabbed their weapon and fled off west through the nearby woods. (IWM BU6601)

deployed 85 metres to the south-east beside the Laison's dried-up northern course, while the remaining Wasp positioned itself between the other two. The commander's Wasp then advanced south-west along a tree-lined grass track toward the 'first' German machine gun nest, located 100 metres beyond the le Roquet road, 110 metres to the north-west of this stand. The Wasp's jets of flame soon dispatched both this nest and the more distant 'second' machine gun (260 metres from the road at what, in 1944, was the end of this tree-line). Meanwhile, the southern Wasp advanced across the fields by the northernmost bank of the Laison. This vehicle then knocked out the 'third' machine gun nest, 190 metres south-west of the le Roquet road, with a burst of flame delivered from 50 metres. On the axis between these actions, the remaining Wasp, hampered by the deep roadside ditch, halted on the edge of the road and flamed at 100 metres the German trenches that covered the bridge. With all four German machine guns accounted for – the crew of the 'fourth' weapon had meanwhile fled – B Company attacked toward both bridges. Within 15 minutes the infantry, having mopped up any remaining German soldiers that had not retreated from the fearsome Wasps, had secured both bridges.

Stand D4: The Bloody Battle for Hill 168.

DIRECTIONS: Return to the Point 93 crossroads and turn left onto the D261 heading west for 1 km. Turn left at Point 103 onto the D261a, continue for 3.8 km, then (600 metres north-east of Soulangy) turn left onto the D246 (signposted Épaney) for 800 metres. Turn right at Point 168 onto a gravel track. Head south for 450 metres past a copse on the left and park by the track crossroads at Point 164. Walk east up the track for 600 metres until a west–east tree-hedge ('the First Hedge'), from which a cut-down hedge ('the Long Hedge') runs south.

ORIENTATION: Face south at the current western end of 'the First Hedge' (which in 1944 extended further west through to Point 164) looking along the 600-metre axis of the recently felled 'Long Hedge'. To the south are visible the exposed fields of la Couture Morel that run toward the 'summit' of Hill 168 1.5 km away (this misleading 1944 term – the terrain is so flat that any peak is imperceptible – refers to the 167.5 metres contour line). Also visible 500 metres to the south-east is a large farm warehouse, while 450 metres beyond this trees obscure the hamlet of le Val Mauger, located in a defile. A single isolated tree, 1 km to the south-southwest, marks the southern end of a recently felled tree-hedge line ('the Far Hedge'), the remains of which – raised ground – extend north for 450 metres from this point. This tree stands adjacent to the track that runs east from Point 159 to Point 160, which formed the objective of this operation.

THE ACTION: From noon on 15 August, Lt-Col Lendrum's 1st Canadian Scottish readied itself for the assault on Objective 'Idaho', the dominating high ground of Hill 168, 4 km north of Falaise. This infantry battalion, supported by some 1st Hussars' Shermans, was to advance south across 1.4 km of exposed ground from its positions along the Soulangy–Épaney road (the modern D246) at Sur le Mont. The 1st Canadian Scottish now redeployed around the farm into a 'box' formation, with its supporting tanks positioned further north. B Company, led that day by Captain D.V. Pugh, plus Major L.S. Henderson's D Company, deployed forward along the western and eastern axes, respectively, while C and A Companies formed-up north of the farm. Unfortunately for the 1st Canadian Scottish, the Germans they were to engage included the fanatical infantry of 3rd Battalion, 26th SS Regiment, who were supported by the fire-power provided by nine panzers. In addition, the Canadian Scottish would have to fight themselves forward across exposed terrain with just their own organic firepower and that provided by the Shermans, since the previous day's rapid advance had taken them beyond the range of effective artillery support. This unpalatable combination of factors led Lendrum to fear that this mission would prove to be a particularly difficult one.

View taken from Stand D4 looking south along the 600-metre-long axis of the recently-felled 'Long Hedge' that bisected the exposed fields of la Couture Morel. The objective of the 1st Canadian Scottish attack – the track 1 km distant which crossed the northern fringes of the 'summit' of Hill 168 – is in the right background, in front of the white buildings. *(Author)*

At 1300 hours, B and D Companies – each with two platoons deployed forward – struck south across the open fields of le Castillon (to the rear of this stand), while A Company followed up 500 metres behind. The infantry's first objective was to cross 500 metres of open ground to reach 'the First Hedge', which lined the track along the southern boundary of these fields. As B and D Companies advanced across le Castillon, they encountered intense defensive fire that inflicted a steady flow of casualties. Two machine guns positioned along 'the First Hedge' – and a further two located west of 'the Long Hedge', which ran south for 600 metres through the fields of la Couture Morel – raked the ground with deadly metal. A few minutes later, mortars and machine guns to the east also began to strike Henderson's D Company with enfilade fire. As if all this was not bad enough, the hard-pressed infantry then saw the advancing Shermans falter and then halt altogether; the armour could not progress any further in the face of accurate fire from two Tigers located to the south-east, plus a third deployed to the south-west. From this point on, the advancing infantry had to make do with the fire support of distant tanks located to the rear rather than the preferable physical and moral presence of Shermans moving forward alongside them.

That afternoon Henderson's D Company fielded several dozen replacements who had not previously seen combat. These inexperienced soldiers now faced an appalling baptism to the realities of war – locked into a frontal assault across open ground against fanatical SS troops, without artillery support or an intimate armoured presence. Not surprisingly, some of them soon went to ground, seeking the largely illusory safety of a hastily scraped hollow in the soil. Indeed, that D Company managed to maintain its forward momentum toward 'the First Hedge' owed much to the professionalism and courage of its officers and NCOs. These leaders set inspirational examples by forging ahead despite the hail of incoming fire, and periodically moving back to exhort men who had gone to ground to advance once more. Yet, even when the two spearhead companies reached 'the First Hedge', their soldiers found no respite from the maelstrom that raged around. The infantrymen soon became embroiled in close-quarter combat with German soldiers located behind this tree-line, which included the two machine-gun crews that had recently dealt out so much death. With this opposition finally cleared, the weary soldiers then formed up on the southern side of the hedge to face the similarly exposed fields of la Couture Morel.

Subsequently, as the remaining men of B and D Companies advanced south across la Couture Morel they encountered another lethal storm of defensive fire. The spearhead of B Company – Acting Sergeant T.W. Bousefield and Sergeant D.W. Robertson's 11 and 12 Platoons advanced south along axes 350 metres west of 'the Long Hedge' and immediately adjacent to this tree-line. Simultaneously, D Company thrust south along an axis between the eastern side of 'the Long Hedge' and the farm warehouse, while A Company followed up behind this unit. As these events unfolded, Captain V.R. Scheldrup's C Company and the battalion headquarters remained deployed around Sur le Mont, where they sustained casualties from accurate German heavy mortar fire. As Robertson's soldiers advanced along both sides of 'the Long Hedge' they flushed out well-concealed snipers, and then overwhelmed two machine guns located at the south-east corner of this tree-line. Robertson then led his soldiers back to the west of the hedge, where they rejoined the bulk of B Company in its advance south.

View from Stand D4 looking south-east across the north-east fringes of la Couture Morel to the farm warehouse, 350 metres away. The courage displayed by two 1st Canadian Scottish NCOs by engaging with PIATs two panzers located 350 metres south of this building was not an isolated incident. Nearby, Private G.L. Thompson bravely worked his way to within 40 metres of a Tiger tank despite being wounded by the tank's machine-gun fire. Next, Thompson scored two successful PIAT hits, which forced the damaged leviathan to withdraw and thus enabled his platoon to resume its advance. *(Author)*

With the entire B Company regrouped, it then pushed south in the face of fierce defensive fire across the track that ran north-east from Point 163 toward the farm warehouse. As it did so, Sergeant Bousefield was wounded but nevertheless continued to lead his platoon. Meanwhile, as D Company advanced to the east of B Company, German machine guns inflicted heavy casualties upon the unit. To reinforce the dwindling power of this eastern thrust, Lendrum now ordered A Company to move up and thrust south on an axis 150 metres east of D Company that passed either side of the warehouse. As A Company advanced south past this building it was fired on by six tanks located in the orchards – long since cleared – located 350 metres west of the north-south tree-line that shrouds the view of le Val Mauger obtainable from this stand. Two Canadian NCOs courageously engaged the tanks with PIAT launchers, and forced them to withdraw. Just prior to this, Lendrum had lost contact with his spearhead forces after German mortar fire had put his headquarters out of action. Consequently, A Company's headquarters assumed the role of a forward battalion tactical headquarters after taking up positions in another orchard located west of le Val Mauger; just a few minutes previously, several PIAT rounds fired by A Company soldiers had driven out three panzers located in this orchard.

From 1630 hours, these three companies determinedly fought their way forward past Point 167 toward their objective, the track that ran across the northern fringe of the summit of Hill 168. In the process, D Company's soldiers crossed over to the western side of the 'Far Hedge'. By 1715 hours, the exhausted remnants of these three units, recently reinforced with elements from Scheldrup's previously uncommitted C Company, had finally secured the battalion's objective. Over the next three hours, what remained of the battalion established firm defensive positions along a 600-metre frontage beside this track. Sadly, the 1st Canadian Scottish paid a high price for this success, caused in part by the fanaticism displayed by the defending SS troops. Many of the Germans eschewed opportunities to surrender and thus died at their posts; in one case when the Canadians overran a trench, an SS trooper put his pistol into his mouth and took his own life rather than be captured. That six members of the 1st Canadian Scottish were recommended for awards rightly reflected the bravery the battalion's personnel displayed that afternoon in securing their objective despite these particularly unfavourable tactical conditions. Indeed, this action was the striking accomplishment of a prematurely-terminated Tractable offensive that failed overall to achieve the degree of success anticipated by Simonds.

No fewer than 33 soldiers of 1st Canadian Scottish paid this ultimate price during the battalion's courageous assault on Hill 168. The battalion only secured its objective after a brutal four-hour battle during which it incurred appalling losses: of the 380 soldiers committed, 159 became casualties. *(NAC PA-132731)*

ENDING THE TOUR: Continue south from the parking spot for 1 km, then turn left at Point 159 onto a grass track and head east for 800 metres (past the isolated tree at the southern end of the former 'Far Hedge'). Turn right/south-east at Point 160 and after 350 metres turn right by les Bruyères onto the D247. Continue for 2 km (passing over the N158) and then turn right at the crossroads in St-Pierre-Canivet. Go north on the D658 for 1.8 km, then right/east for 900 metres (again passing over the N158). Take the left-hand fork to join the N158 and return to Caen.

PART FOUR

ON YOUR
RETURN

FURTHER RESEARCH

Once participants on these tours have returned home, they may find their interest so stimulated that they wish to find out more about these events; indeed, this may also be true even if the individual has read this work but not yet set off for the Caen–Falaise area, or else only intends to experience these tours from the comfort of an armchair. The obvious first place to start further research into Operations Totalize and Tractable is to consult published secondary sources. Some of these focus just on some actions within these battles such as Ken Tout, *The Bloody Battle for Tilly*, (Stroud, Sutton, 2000) and Les Taylor, 'Michael Wittmann's Last Battle' in *After the Battle* (No. 48, 1985, pp. 46–53). For books that examine the wider Normandy campaign as well as covering these operations, consult: Terry Copp, *Fields of Fire: The Canadians in Normandy* (London, University of Toronto Press, 2003); L.F. Ellis, *Victory in the West*, Vol. 1, (History of the Second World War, UK Military Series), (London, HMSO, 1962); John A. English, *The Canadian Army and the Normandy Campaign: A Study in the Failure of High Command*, (London, Praeger, 1991); Stephen A. Hart, *Montgomery and 'Colossal Cracks', the 21st Army Group in Northwest Europe 1944–45*, (London, Praeger, 2001); and C.P. Stacey, *The Victory Campaign*, (Official History of the Canadian Army in the Second World War, Vol. 3), (Ottawa, The Queen's Printer, 1960).

For published divisional and unit histories, try: Alastair Borthwick, *Battalion: A British Infantry Unit's Actions from El Alamein to the Elbe, 1942–1945*, (London, Bâton Wicks, 1994); Donald E. Graves, *S. Albertas: A Canadian Regiment at War*, (Toronto, Robin Brass, 1998); Hubert Meyer, *History of the 12-SS Panzer Division 'Hitlerjugend'*, (Winnipeg, J.J. Fedorowicz, 1994) – originally published as *Kriegsgeschichte der 12. SS-Panzerdivision 'Hitlerjugend'*, (Osnabrück, Munin Verlag, 1982); and J.B. Salmond, *The History of the 51st Highland Division*, (Edinburgh, Wm. Blackwood, 1953). In terms of published memoirs, the following are well worth consulting: George

Above: A convoy headed by a Canadian armoured car passes an abandoned German *Sturmgeschütz* III assault gun. *(NAC PA-169068)*

Page 185: Close-up of Mont-Royal Fusilier Leo Benoit near Bretteville-sur-Laize, 10 August 1944. The protracted fighting around May-sur-Orne had been so intense that Benoit had not been able even to have a shave. *(NAC PA-132905)*

Kitching, *Mud & Green Fields: The Memoirs of Major General Kitching*, (Langley, B.C., Battleline, 1986); and Kurt Meyer, *Grenadiers*, (Winnipeg, J.J. Fedorowicz, 1994). In addition, relevant biographies include: Dominick Graham, *The Price of Command: The Biography of General Guy G. Simonds*, (Toronto, Stoddart, 1993); and Tony Foster, *A Meeting of Generals*, (Toronto, Methuen, 1986) (which relates to Kurt Meyer). Finally, for an examination of the fanaticism displayed by *Hitlerjugend* soldiers, see Stephen A. Hart, 'Indoctrinated Nazi teenaged warriors: the fanaticism of the 12th SS Panzer Division *Hitlerjugend* in Normandy, 1944' in M. Hughes and

G. Johnson (eds.), *Fanaticism and Conflict in the Modern Age*, (London, Frank Cass, 2004).

For those wishing to consult primary documents relating to these battles the obvious place to start would be the British National Archives (formerly known as the Public Record Office, in Kew, southwest London) and the National Archives of Canada (in Ottawa). In both archives individuals can view the extensive range of original war diaries and operational papers that this author consulted in producing this work. It should be noted, however, that some contemporary Canadian documents that were never duplicated may be missing from the files housed at the National Archives (in series WO179), and are thus only to be found in Ottawa. At the National Archives, readers should consult document classes WO171 (for British war diaries), and WO179 (for Canadian war diaries), as well as the useful post-war battlefield tour located at CAB 106/1047. In Ottawa, relevant materials are to be found in Record Group 24 and the Crerar Papers. Finally, for those interested in the Allied and German tank designs that participated in the battle fought in front of Falaise, some of these can be viewed at the Tank Museum at Bovington, Dorset, UK, together with original papers relating to their development. The last word to say on further research, is that if all these sources have not quenched your desire to know more about these fascinating Normandy battles, then the bibliographies and other guidance contained or referred to in these sources will undoubtedly have given you more leads to pursue in the quest truly to understand the II Canadian Corps' August 1944 Totalize and Tractable offensives. Happy researching!

Useful Addresses

UK National Archives, Public Record Office, Kew, Richmond, Surrey TW9 4DU; tel: 020 8876 3444; email: <enquiry@nationalarchives.gov.uk>; web: <www.nationalarchives.gov.uk>.

Imperial War Museum, Lambeth Road, London SE1 6HZ; tel: 020 7416 5320; email: <mail@iwm.org.uk>; web: <www.iwm.org.uk>.

Public Archives of Canada, 395 Wellington Street, Ottawa, Ontario K1A 0N3; tel: +01 613 9470 391.

Tank Museum, Bovington, Dorset BH20 6JG; tel: 01929 405096; web: <www.tankmuseum.co.uk>.

ON YOUR RETURN

INDEX

Page numbers in *italics* denote an illustration.

Adams, Lt Gerry 64
air support 20–1, 22, 49, 50, 56, 77, 84, 89, 163
aircraft:
  Avro Lancaster 95, 138
  Boeing B-17 Flying Fortress 50, *51*
  Handley Page Halifax 95
  Hawker Typhoon fighter-bomber 77, 163
Always, Lt-Col B.M. 36, 37
Andrews, Lt-Col G.L.W. 'Geordie' 46, 146, 148, 149
Argentan 17, 81
armoured vehicles, Allied:
  AVRE fascine-carriers 94, 95, 173, 175
  Churchill tanks 61, 97
  Crocodile flame-throwers 22, 97, 98, 140–2, *141*
  Firefly, 17-pdr Shermans 57, 58, *107*, 156, 158
  M3A1 White scout car 15, *187*
  M4 Shermans *3, 13*, 36, 58, 60, 64–5, 65, 75, 76, 83, 90, 92, *93*, *123*, 133–4, 156, 158, 161, *172*, 181
  M10 Wolverine tank destroyers 97
  Priest, M7 self-propelled howitzers 23, 127, *128*, 133
  Ram artillery observation tank 56
  Sherman Crab flails *13*, 35, 42, *123*, 130
  Wasp flame-throwing Bren carriers 96, 177–9, *178*
armoured vehicles, German:
  Panzer IV 127
  Panzer V Panthers 20, 127, 161
  Panzer VI Tigers 53, 55, 58, 75, 155–9, 177, 181
  Sturmgeschütz III assault guns 55, *187*
Armstrong, L/Cpl Tom 79
artillery:
  Allied:
    40-mm Bofors 34, 36, 37, 122
    towed 17-pdr anti-tank guns 78, 92, 129, 146
  German: 88-mm flak/anti-tank guns 33, 65
  Assy 84, 94, 96, 98, 175, 177

Balogh, Pte J.A. *113*
Barnes, Sgt *150*

barrage, creeping 28, 36, 121, 130, 146
Beauvoir Farm 35, 38, *119*, 121, 136
Benoit, Fus Leo *185*
Bochniak, Warrant Officer Adolf *155*
Booth, Brig Leslie 62, 69
Bourguébus 14, 15, 18, 19, 27, 31, 45, *130*
Bousefield, A/Sgt T.W. 182, 183
Bradley, Lt Gen Omar N. 17
Breitmoser, *SS-Unterscharführer* Kurt 79
Bretteville-le-Rabet 29, 62, 69, 71, 74, 75, 76, 80
Bretteville-sur-Laize 20, 30, 50, 51, 52, 58
British Army:
  Second Army 16, 81
  Divisions: 51st (Highland) 24, 26, 30, 41, 45, 83, 102
  Brigades:
    33rd Armoured 24, 41
    152nd Infantry 27, 45, 149
    153rd Infantry 26, 45–6
    154th Infantry 41
  Armour:
    141st Regiment Royal Armoured Corps 98, 140, 142
    144th Regiment Royal Armoured Corps 42, 156, 158
    148th Regiment Royal Armoured Corps 42, 44, 151
    1st Lothian and Border Yeomanry 35
    1st Northamptonshire Yeomanry 42, 58, 66, *107*, 130, 156
  Royal Artillery, Army Group (AGRA) 30, 80
  Royal Engineers: 80th Assault Squadron 95, 173, 175
  Infantry Battalions:
    7th Argyll and Sutherland Highlanders 42
    1st Black Watch 23, 42, 130
    7th Black Watch 42, 44
    5th Cameron Highlanders 27, 46–7
    1st Gordon Highlanders 26
    1st/7th Middlesex Regiment 146
    2nd Seaforth Highlanders 27, 45, 146, 150
    5th Seaforth Highlanders 28, 149, 151

Caillouet 25, 31–2, 35, *124*, *125*, 128–9
Canadian Army:
  First Army *18*, 19, 81, 82
  Corps: II Corps 14, 18, 19, 21, 80, 82, 102, 104–5, 137, 163

Divisions:
  2nd Infantry 19, 24–6, 30, 102, 105, 136
  3rd Infantry 19, 30, 80, 83, 85, 87, 105, 169
  4th Armoured 29–30, 62, 83, 86, 105, 169
Brigades:
  2nd Armoured 24, *53*, 80, 85, 93, 97, 98, 104
  4th Armoured 12, 26, 59, 64–5, 67–8, 69, 71, 73, 76, 86, 97, 162–3, 169, 172
  4th Infantry 35
  6th Infantry 25, 37, 136
  7th Infantry 85
  8th Infantry 80, 86, 87, 98, 171
  9th Infantry 85, 92, 96
  10th Infantry 86, 87, 98, 171
Battlegroups:
  Halpenny Force 59, 62, 69, 71, 74
  Worthington Force 69, 70–4, 71, 79–80, 96, 108, 160–5, *160*
Armour:
  6th Canadian (1st Hussars) 38, 85, 90, 93, *93*, 94–5, 99, 173, 175, 179
  7th Reconnaissance (Duke of York's Royal Canadian Hussars) 85, 93, 96
  8th Reconnaissance (14th Hussars) 25, 36, 121, 128
  10th Canadian (Fort Garry Horse) *13*, 35, 36, 83, 85, 90, 93, 95, 98–9, 102
  21st Canadian (Governor General's Foot Guards) 74–5, 78, 86, 97, 99, 101, 103, 104, 163, 171
  22nd Canadian (Canadian Grenadier Guards) 59, 62, 74, 75–6, 80, 86, 97, 99, 101, 103–4, 163, 171
  27th Canadian (Sherbrooke Fusiliers) 35, 156, 158
  28th Canadian (British Columbia Regiment) 71, 86, 99, 101, 103, 160, 163, 171
  29th Reconnaissance (South Alberta Regiment) 64, 65, 70, 74, 76, 77, 87, 101, 171
Royal Canadian Artillery: 2nd Army Group (AGRA) 80
Infantry Battalions:
  Algonquin Regiment 71, 75, 101, 102, 103, 160
  Argyll and Sutherland Highlanders of Canada 64, 65, 74, 76, 77–8, 101
  Cameron Highlanders of Canada 38